The Diamond Rule:
Secrets of a
Master Diamond Cutter

By Dr. Nate Booth
with Dr. Steve Price

INTI
PUBLISHING

Your Personal Growth Is Our Personal Mission

The Diamond Rule:
Secrets of a
Master Diamond Cutter

intipublishing.com

The Diamond Rule: Secrets of a Master Diamond Cutter

By Dr. Nate Booth with Dr. Steve Price

Copyright © 2001 by Dr. Nate Booth and Dr. Steve Price

Printed in the United States of America

First edition June, 2001

ISBN: 1-891279-07-6

Published by INTI Publishing, Inc.

Tampa, FL

Cover Design: CherryDesign

Layout: Parry Design Studio

intipublishing.com

DEDICATION

To everyone who has ever wished
they could make a bad relationship better...
or a good relationship great.

ABOUT THIS BOOK

Much of the material in *The Diamond Rule: Secrets of a Master Diamond Cutter* is taken verbatim from *The Diamond Touch*, an original book by Dr. Nate Booth published in 1998 by Harrison Acorn Press.

The purpose in publishing *The Diamond Rule: Secrets of a Master Diamond Cutter* was to streamline Dr. Booth's original material; to focus the message on the importance of relationships; and to make a parallel between how Master Diamond Cutters increase the value of rough diamonds and how Master Relationship Builders improve the quality of their relationships.

The author(s) or publisher(s) apologize in advance for any confusion that may be caused by the re-publication of selected material from *The Diamond Touch*.

ABOUT THE AUTHORS

Dr. Nate Booth was in private dental practice for eight years before he decided to switch careers. Today, Dr. Booth creates customized training programs for corporations and associations around the world.

Dr. Booth and his wife, Dawn, have three children: Chris, age 35; Emily, age 25; and Belinda, age 16. Dr. Booth, Dawn, and Belinda live in Encinitas, California.

Dr. Steve Price, a former English teacher, received his doctorate in English from Illinois State University in 1985. To date he has co-authored more than a dozen books on personal growth and free enterprise.

Dr. Price lives and works in Tampa, Florida. His 10-year-old daughter, Sydney, is an avid reader and budding author.

WHY I WROTE THIS BOOK

The driving force behind this book can be summed up in one short sentence:

Relationships are the most valuable possessions in our lives and deserve to be treated accordingly.

Think about the value of your relationships for a moment. Everything we do... every decision we make... every feeling we feel... every joy we experience... every disappointment we suffer... has its root in a relationship.

Relationships are far more valuable than money—that's obvious. Would you trade a great relationship with your child or your parents for a million dollars? Ten million? A billion? NO WAY! Relationships are literally priceless!

Relationships are even more valuable than your health... even more valuable than your life, for that matter. Think about it—why did the Pilgrims risk their lives to settle an unexplored wilderness we now call America? So that they could have the freedom to nurture their relationship with God... their families... and with their fellow Pilgrims, that's why.

Yes, relationships are our most valuable possession. Yet most of us have never been taught how to grow and improve our relationships, isn't that true? We just blunder along, often doing more harm than good, damaging our relationships not out of malice, but out of ignorance.

That's why I wrote this book!

I wanted to share some simple yet powerful strategies that can empower people to dramatically increase the value of their most precious possession—their relationships! This book will give you the information and the know-how that will enable you to transform your relationships from "diamonds in the rough"... to sparkling gems.

You, too, can become a Master Diamond Cutter. It's easier than you think. All you need to do is to set aside a couple of hours to read this book... and then to apply the strategies of a Master Diamond Cutter to the relationships in your life.

Remember, diamonds are valuable.

But relationships... *are priceless!*

CONTENTS

Introduction

The Power of
Practicing the
Diamond Rule

The Power of Practicing the Diamond Rule

With all thy getting, get understanding.
—Proverbs

he Master Diamond Cutter stood over the biggest diamond in the world. He made a fist and placed it next to the diamond... then shook his head in disbelief.

The diamond and his fist were the same size!

The most memorable event in the 2,500-year history of the diamond trade was about to occur—the cutting of the monstrous Cullinan Diamond. The date was February 10, 1907. The place, Amsterdam, Holland.

The job of the Master Diamond Cutter, Joseph Asscher, was to split the Cullinan in such a way as to maximize its value. This was no easy task. In a diamond the size of the Cullinan, the wrong split could reduce the value by hundreds of millions of dollars! *Talk about pressure…!*

For six months Asscher had been studying the Cullinan, searching for the best fault line along which to cleave the diamond. He knew every curve of the Cullinan. Every crease. Every wrinkle. But no matter how long the Master Diamond Cutter studied the monster diamond, he still marveled at its size.

The Cullinan was so big that it dwarfed the world's previous biggest diamond, the Excelsior, which weighed 995.2 carats, or about seven ounces, in the rough. The Cullinan weighed an astronomical 3,016 carats, which calculates to *about a pound and a half!*

But today the studying was over for the Master Diamond Cutter.

Today was the day of reckoning.

Today was the day the world's greatest diamond cutter would cleave the world's biggest diamond.

The Master Diamond Cutter had marked the angle of the cut on the Cullinan in India ink. He'd notched the surface where he would place his cleaving steel. The expert witnesses were gathered in his studio.

The Master Diamond Cutter pressed his cleaving steel against the giant gem.

He raised his mallet above his head.

And as sudden as a startled breath, the mallet struck the steel with a thud!

The witnesses blinked in unison at the impact... then rushed forward to examine the fate of the biggest diamond in the world. They stared at the cleaved Cullinan in amazement... Joseph Asscher, the Master Diamond Cutter, had lived up to his reputation! *The greatest diamond cutter in the world had split the greatest diamond in the world perfectly!*

The Greatest Gem of All Time

When all the shaping and polishing were completed, "the greatest gem of all time" produced the two largest polished diamonds in the world, Cullinan I and II. These and seven other of the largest stones from the Cullinan became part of the British Crown Jewels. The King of England ordered Cullinan I to be added to the royal scepter. Cullinan II was set in the front of the Royal Crown.

If it weren't for the skill of the Master Diamond Cutter, Joseph Asscher, the story of the Cullinan Diamond could have turned out very differently.

But Asscher was up to the challenge. By applying his skill and knowledge, he brought out the best in the Cullinan, transforming it from a milky-colored, lopsided chunk of stone weighing a pound and a half into 107 flawless gems fit for royalty.

DIAMOND CUTTING IS A LOT LIKE RELATIONSHIP BUILDING

The Master Diamond Cutter's job is to increase the value of a diamond in the rough by bringing out its best natural features. You see, Master Diamond Cutters practice *"The Diamond Rule"*—they seek to discover the uniqueness inherent in each rough diamond, and then they bring out the diamond's full value by cutting and shaping with the natural grain, instead of against it.

When you think about it, diamond cutting is a lot like relationship building. Relationships start off as "diamonds in the rough." Like diamonds, each person is one of a kind and has his or her own unique "grain." Master Relationship Builders recognize each person's unique grain and then bring out the best in their relationship by working *with* the grain, instead of against it.

THE DIAMOND RULE AND RELATIONSHIPS

The Diamond Rule applies to relationship building, just as much as it applies to diamond cutting. We've all heard of the "Golden Rule"—treat others as *you* want to be treated. The Golden Rule is a great rule.

▲

The Diamond Rule says, "Treat others as they uniquely want to be treated!"

▼

But the Diamond Rule is even better. The Diamond Rule says, "Treat others as *they* **uniquely** want to be treated!"

Just as a pound of diamonds is far more valuable than a pound of gold, the Diamond Rule is far more valuable than the Golden Rule! Why? Because the Diamond Rule is designed to recognize and honor the uniqueness of each person. And when we learn to do that, the value of our relationships will skyrocket!

When you practice the Diamond Rule in all your relationships, you'll develop the *"Diamond Touch"* of a Master Diamond Cutter. And once you have the Diamond Touch, you'll know exactly what to say and do to foster understanding... facilitate cooperation... heighten harmony... increase loyalty... and engender trust in all your relationships.

As a result, you'll enjoy more success in your business, more love in your family, and more happiness in your life. *That's the power of practicing the Diamond Rule!*

Section 1

Diamonds Are Expensive... but Relationships Are Priceless!

Section 1

Diamonds Are Expensive... but Relationships Are Priceless!

Let's Review:

In the Introduction you learned learned how a Master Diamond Cutter was able to increase the value of the giant Cullinan Diamond *from millions to BILLIONS* by practicing the Diamond Rule, that is, the Master Diamond Cutter released the rough diamond's full value by cutting and shaping the diamond with its natural grain, instead of working against it.

You also learned the difference between the Golden Rule (treat others as YOU would like to be treated) and the Diamond Rule (treat others in the <u>unique way</u> THEY would like to be treated); and you learned that diamond cutting is like relationship building—the only way to bring out the full value of a diamond or a relationship is to practice the Diamond Rule.

What's Ahead:

In the coming section you will learn why diamonds have become the most valuable natural mineral and why relationships are far more valuable than all of the diamonds in the world.

CHAPTER 1

Why Diamonds Are the "King of Gems"!

◇

*Next to good judgment, diamonds are the
rarest things in the world.*
—Anonymous

Diamonds are in a class by themselves. And they always have been since they were first discovered in India more than 2,500 years ago.

Call it the "diamond mystique."

The ancient Greeks revered diamonds, thinking they were splinters of stars that had fallen to Earth. In the Middle Ages, only kings and noblemen were allowed to wear diamonds. In the Victorian Age, rich businessmen showed off their wealth by buying diamond tie pins for themselves and diamond necklaces for their wives.

The diamond mystique has not lost any of its luster over the centuries. Today diamonds are used to commemorate special occasions, such as engagements and 60th wedding anniversaries. Or to designate special achievements.

"Diamonds are forever," says the advertising slogan for DeBeers, the world's largest miner and distributor of diamonds. Diamonds symbolize the ultimate in rank... achievement... wealth... beauty... and excellence. Diamonds represent the best. The top. The pinnacle. The ultimate. Yes, diamonds are forever.

Think about it this way—if you could be any gem in the world, which one would you want to be?

A diamond, of course!

WHAT'S BEHIND THE DIAMOND MYSTIQUE?

How can something that looks like a dull glass pebble in its natural state and is composed entirely of one of the most common substances in the world—carbon—be assigned such *uncommon value and status?*

The unique combination of rarity, durability, and beauty is what makes diamonds so valuable. So valuable, in fact, that every other precious metal and gem pales in comparison to diamonds, including gold. An ounce of gold, for example, is worth about $250 today. A one-ounce diamond, on the other hand, would weigh 30 carats and could cost millions! Which means diamonds are thousands of times more valuable than gold!

Let's take a closer look at the unique traits that make diamonds so valuable. Let's start by talking about one of the oldest axioms of value—the law of supply and demand. In the case of diamonds, there is a lot of demand but little supply. Thus, the prices remain high. If diamonds were as plentiful as gravel, they would fetch the same price as gravel. But diamonds are *rare*. In fact, they are the rarest mineral in the world. A mining company must excavate 5,000 tons of rock to find one carat of diamonds, and only 20% of those are gem quality.

Another reason diamonds are so valuable is their *hardness*. The carbon atoms in diamonds are combined in such a way as to create a crystal that's 140 times harder than the next hardest natural substance, corundum. The diamond got its name because of its extraordinary hardness—the word diamond comes from the Greek word *adamas,* meaning "invincible" or "unconquerable."

A final reason that diamonds are deemed so valuable is their *beauty*. No other substance has the sparkle and shine of diamonds. When light hits a cut and polished diamond, the flat surfaces act as a mirror, reflecting the light to create a brilliant "fire" that is unique to diamonds. This is where the Master Diamond Cutter comes into play. You see, diamonds in their natural state are lopsided and uneven and often have a dull, oily appearance. The job of a Master Diamond

Cutter is to release a diamond's hidden beauty by cleaving it into smaller rough-cut gems, and then cutting, shaping, and polishing them into sparkling gems.

THE POWER OF THE DIAMOND TOUCH

Diamonds in their natural state are valuable, that goes without saying. But the amazing thing about diamonds is that their value can be multiplied 10 times… 100 times… even 1,000 times in the hands of a Master Diamond Cutter. Unfortunately, the opposite is also true. An unskilled diamond cutter can dramatically diminish the value of a rough diamond.

Joseph Asscher, the Master Diamond Cutter, had the Diamond Touch because he could *literally* transform a "diamond in the rough" worth *millions*… into dozens of polished gems worth *billions*.

▲

… the expression "Diamond Touch" refers to anyone who has the know how to bring out the best in something or someone.

▼

Fortunately, the Diamond Touch isn't limited to just diamonds and other precious gems. Just as the expression "a diamond in the rough" refers to a person with great potential who lacks polish and refinement, the expression "Diamond Touch" refers to anyone who has the know how to bring out the best in something or someone.

For example, if you owned a Formula One race car, who would you want to tune up the engine in preparation for the Indy 500? Your teenage son? Or a master mechanic with the Diamond Touch? If you owned the Chicago Bulls basketball team when Michael Jordan was playing, who would you want to coach your team? A hot-headed fan in the third row? Or Phil Jackson, a master coach with the Diamond Touch?

Here's my point: When I talk about someone having the Diamond Touch, it means they have learned the "secrets" of their trade, that is, they have acquired the specialized tools and gained the specialized knowledge that enable them to bring out the best in others.

APPLYING THE DIAMOND TOUCH TO YOUR RELATIONSHIPS

Now, let me ask you a couple of questions: Wouldn't you agree that trusting, meaningful, dependable relationships are more valuable than diamonds? And wouldn't it be great if you could apply the Diamond Touch to the most precious possession in your life—your relationships?

When you think about it, our relationships are like diamonds in the rough—they need to be cut and shaped and polished to bring out their full beauty and potential. If anything deserves to be handled with a Diamond Touch, it's our relationships.

If anything deserves to be handled with a Diamond Touch, it's our relationships.

Truth is, very few people have received any specialized training in relationship building. I've attended four years of high school and nine years of college, and I've never had the opportunity to take a course in relationship building. I doubt that you have either.

Let's face it, *when it comes to building relationships, most people are rank amateurs!* Yet we're turned loose to cut and shape the rough diamonds in our lives, our relationships. Is it an wonder that so many of our relationships end up damaged, maybe even splintered and shattered, as a result?

Think about the relationships in your life—are some of your relationships "rough around the edges"? Do some need smoothing and polishing? Are some a bit out of round? Are others dull and lackluster, even though you'd like them to sparkle? And have some of your relationships been so badly cleaved and shaped that their full value will never be fully realized?

YOU CAN BECOME A MASTER DIAMOND CUTTER

Why are our relationships less than perfect? Because, unlike Master Diamond Cutters, we've never been taught the "secrets" to cutting and shaping our relationships.

Wouldn't it be great to learn the "secrets" of a Master Diamond Cutter so that you could bring out the full potential of your relationships?

Wouldn't it be great to be able to shape and polish your relationships with your spouse... your children... your co-workers... and every new person you meet so that they sparkle and shine like gems?

Well, now you, too, can have the Diamond Touch!

The "secrets" of a Master Diamond Cutter are right at your fingertips. These secrets are time-tested and can be applied to virtually any relationship. Best of all, the secrets of a Master Diamond Cutter are simple and easy to learn and apply. But they're as powerful as the cleaving steel that split the Cullinan Diamond!

Let's turn to the next chapter to begin learning the strategies and techniques of a Master Diamond Cutter so that we can begin to transform our relationships from diamonds in the rough... to sparkling gems!

CHAPTER 2

Relationships:
The Gems of
Our Lives

*Mastering relationships is simple... treat every person
you meet as the most important person in your life.*
—George W. Cummings, Sr.
from "Lessons at the Fence Post"

ictionary definition:
Priceless (pris´lis) *adj.* 1. of inestimable value;
beyond price.

We often hear the word "priceless" used to describe
great art, such as the *Mona Lisa* by Leonardo da Vinci. But truth is,
every *thing* has a price. The price may be astronomical. But under the
right circumstances, the Cullinan Diamonds and the *Mona Lisa* can
be bought.

That's just not the case with relationships. Our most precious relationships are, indeed, priceless. No amount of money could ever replace a beloved spouse… a precious child… or a dear friend. Even the coldest, shrewdest businessmen in history have valued their relationships more than their money.

It's true!

Aristotle Onassis, for example, was a greedy, cold-hearted, calculating businessman if there ever was one. Heartless was the one word most often used to describe him.

But as hard-hearted as Onassis was, he was grief stricken when his only son died in an airplane crash. The Greek tycoon never recovered from the loss of his beloved son. Onassis lost the will to live and died two years after his son's funeral.

Do you think Aristotle Onassis—shrewd, cold-hearted businessman that he was—would have traded all of his wealth for his son's life? *In a New York minute!*

Personal Relationships Are Priceless Gems

If the loss of a loved one has the power to drive a cold-hearted creature like Aristotle Onassis to an early grave, just think how the loss of a family member would affect the average person. It just reminds us that relationships have to be right at the top of the list of things that are more important than money!

Why are relationships so important to us? Well, first and foremost, humans are social animals. People need to be around other people. We weren't meant to be hermits. Relationships define who we are and how we feel about ourselves and the world around us.

That's why solitary confinement is such an effective punishment. When you isolate people, you cut them off from the vine. And when people are cut from the vine, they begin to die....

As John Maxwell points out in his classic bestseller, *Be A People Person,* "The least important word [in the English language] is I. The most important word—*we.*"

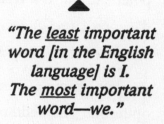

"The least important word [in the English language] is I. The most important word—we."

Just look at the people around you. I think you'd agree that the happiest, most fulfilled people you know are the ones who are successful at building great relationships. Master Relationship Builders have happy marriages. Raise well-adjusted, well-behaved children. Create deep, long-lasting friendships. Enjoy profitable businesses. And have positive self-esteem and lots of self-confidence. In short, Master Relationship Builders possess more of the good things in life—more love... more laughter... more intimacy... more harmony... and more passion—while enduring less of the negative emotions that wear people down, such as stress... anger... tension... and conflict.

TRANSFORMING ROUGH RELATIONSHIPS INTO QUALITY GEMS

I once heard a minister say that relationships are like eggs. An egg has to be *transformed* before it can fly. If the egg isn't transformed, it goes bad.

Same thing with relationships. Each relationship starts off as an "egg." If it hatches and is nurtured properly, it soars to its full potential. But if a relationship is abandoned as an egg, then it will die... or if a relationship is neglected or abused during its stay in the nest, then it will become stunted and deformed.

For example, every marriage starts off with great promise and optimism. The wedding vows portend a loving, long-lasting relationship: "For richer or for poorer... in sickness and in health... 'til death do us part."

Unfortunately, the relationship between many husbands and wives deteriorates over time. Gradually, the partners start bringing out the worst in each other, instead of the best. The relationship becomes strained with anger... ripe with unfulfilled emotional needs... rife with resentment. Little wonder that half the marriages end in divorce.

What goes wrong? What causes so many promising, loving relationships to be transformed into dull, lackluster rocks... instead of sparkling, valuable gems?

THE DIAMOND RULE VS. THE GOLDEN RULE

What goes wrong is that one or both people in the relationship aren't aware of the Diamond Rule. Everyone is familiar with the Golden Rule: "Treat others as *you* would like to be treated." The Diamond Rule is similar to the Golden Rule but with one big difference. When you follow the Diamond Rule, you treat each person not as *you* like to be treated, but as *he or she uniquely wants to be treated.* The distinction between how YOU want to be treated and how THEY want to be treated makes a big, BIG difference.

Now, before I go into a discussion of the Diamond Rule, I'd like to make a couple of observations about the Golden Rule. First of all, I want to say that the Golden Rule is a great rule. The Golden Rule is certainly a step in the right direction because it encourages people to put themselves in someone else's place.

But therein lies the problem.

When we put ourselves in someone else's place, we're still seeing things through *our own eyes and feelings!* Which leads us to conclude, "This is how I WOULD FEEL in this situation," or "This is what I WOULD WANT in this situation." Problem is, there's usually a big difference between what you would feel and want in a given situation and what another person would feel and want. A BIG DIFFERENCE!

The Diamond Rule goes one step further than the Golden Rule. The Diamond Rule encourages people to see things not only from the

▲

The Diamond Rule emphasizes THEIR thoughts and feelings and values, instead of YOURS!

▼

other person's point of view, *but through the other person's thoughts and feelings!* In other words, the Diamond Rule emphasizes THEIR thoughts and feelings and values, instead of YOURS!

A CASE STUDY: THE GOLDEN RULE IN ACTION

Here's a true story that illustrates why the Golden Rule can be inadvertently harmful to relationships, whereas the Diamond Rule can bring out the best in our most precious possession, our relationships.

I have a friend named Stan who was engaged to a woman named Mary. On the surface, they seemed like a perfect couple, and they were crazy about each other. Stan expressed his affection by bringing Mary small gifts once or twice a week. Stan loved receiving little gifts and surprises, so he assumed that everyone else would feel the same as he did. So by practicing the Golden Rule—treating others as he would like to be treated—Stan assumed Mary would love getting little, unsolicited tokens of his affection.

Wrong assumption! Mary did NOT like receiving regular gifts from Stan. You see, money and material things didn't impress Mary very much. In fact, she was anti-materialistic. Mary preferred to drive a 10-year-old car with 200,000 miles on it to buying a new one, even though she could easily afford a new car. Mary liked genuine, salt-of-the-earth people. She hated phonies and status seekers. As a result, Mary interpreted Stan's buying her gifts as a warning sign that

Stan was superficial and irresponsible with money. Plus, she felt he was trying to buy her affection, and she resented it. So every time Mary got a gift from Stan, a red flag went up and her affection went down.

Stan was hurt and confused by Mary's indifference to his gifts. "Any 'normal' woman would love getting surprise gifts," Stan thought to himself. "There must be something seriously wrong with Mary."

GOOD INTENTIONS, BAD RESULTS

The sad part is that Stan and Mary were two great people who could have had a great relationship if they'd only understood and practiced the Diamond Rule, instead of the Golden Rule.

Unfortunately, Stan, like most people, wasn't aware of the Diamond Rule. He honestly thought he was doing the right thing by practicing the Golden Rule. But the more he treated Mary as *he* wanted to be treated (instead of how *she* wanted to be treated), the more Mary backed away. And the more Mary backed away, the more angry and resentful Stan became.

The misunderstandings and suspicions between Stan and Mary kept building to the point that they called off the engagement. The saddest part is that neither Stan nor Mary could ever quite figure out what went wrong in their relationship. She didn't have the heart to tell him that she didn't want his gifts for fear of appearing ungrateful. He didn't see any reason to think that she would resent receiving gifts.

All Stan and Mary knew was that the relationship had deteriorated to the point that they both felt their only option was to end it.

YOU DON'T HAVE TO HURT THE ONE YOU LOVE...

What happened to Stan and Mary happens all the time in relationships. Most people have good intentions, but they inadvertently do or say things that damage their relationships. It's like the old song says, "You always hurt, the one you love. The one you didn't want to hurt at all." Sad... but, all too true.

Think about your own life. Have you ever had an important relationship disintegrate before your eyes, but you could never quite figure out what went wrong? I know I have.

Have you ever said to yourself, "No matter what I do or say, I can never make so-and-so happy." Or, "What do women (or men) really want?" Or, "The harder I try, the worse our relationship gets." Or, "I've given up trying to understand so-and-so. It's like we live on different planets."

Wouldn't it be great if you knew *exactly* what to say and do to bring out the best in people? Wouldn't it be great if you learned the secret that could transform strained relationships into sterling ones?

Well, when you have the Diamond Touch, that's exactly what happens—you learn what others want from you and how they want it. Then all you have to do to increase the value of your relationship is to do what they say! Sounds simple, doesn't it? Well, it *is* simple to learn and apply the Diamond Touch.

You've already taken the first step by learning about the power of the Diamond Rule. Let's take the next step by turning to the next chapter and learning the key questions that will transform your relationships from diamonds in the rough... to sparkling gems!

Section 2

How to Cut and
Shape the Gems
in Your Life

Section 2

How to Cut and Shape the Gems in Your Life

Let's Review:

In the last section, you learned why relationships are more valuable than diamonds... and you learned that the value of relationships can be increased dramatically. You also learned that the key to increasing the value of relationships is to practice the Diamond Rule, that is, to "Treat others in the unique way they want to be treated."

This definition raises two questions:

1. What is it that people really want in life?

2. How can you discover what they really want in life?

What's Ahead:

In the coming section, you'll learn that WHAT people want to experience the most in life are emotions. And the emotions a person wants to experience the most determine that person's VALUES.

If Values are the emotions that people want to experience, then Sparks are the exact way they want to experience those emotions. In order to increase the value of your relationships, you must practice the Diamond Rule; and in order to practice the Diamond Rule, you must discover a person's true Values and their unique Sparks.

CHAPTER 3

Cutting and Shaping Relationships "with the Grain"

The greatest good you can do for another
is not just to share your riches,
but to reveal to him his own.
     —Benjamin Disraeli

ell me what's wrong with the following scenario.

  A new female patient walks into a dental office. The dentist has never met her. Before she opens her mouth, the dentist walks up to her and says, "You need three porcelain crowns on your back teeth, complete orthodontic treatment, and two of your wisdom teeth removed."

It's obvious what's wrong with this scene. The dentist would be prescribing a course of action before doing an examination and diagnosis, and prescription without diagnosis is malpractice. The patient would probably turn around and walk out of the office, and the dentist's license would eventually be revoked.

PRESCRIPTION WITHOUT DIAGNOSIS IS MALPRACTICE.

In my experience of working with thousands of people, I've observed that most people treat others like the clueless dentist treated the new patient—that is, they offer a course of action before doing an examination and diagnosis. In other words, most people treat others according to the Golden Rule (how *they* want to be treated) instead of the Diamond Rule (how the *other person* wants to be treated).

Let me put it another way. What would have happened if Joseph Asscher, the Master Diamond Cutter, had cleaved the Cullinan Diamond the way *he* wanted to, instead of *the way the diamond was naturally inclined?* Asscher could have shattered the diamond, diminishing the value of the Cullinan by hundreds of millions of dollars!

But Asscher understood that every diamond has four natural planes of weakness, or "grains," along which it can be easily cleaved. That's why he studied the Cullinan for six months before he cleaved it. He wanted to make sure that he identified the natural grain and then split the diamond along the grain that would optimize the diamond's value.

EMOTIONS: THE NATURAL GRAIN OF PEOPLE

Like diamonds, people have natural "grains" or tendencies. Whereas diamonds have four cleavage points, humans have five emotional "cleavage" points (we'll identify and discuss the five key emotions in the next chapter). Just as you can't cut and shape a diamond against the grain, you can't "cut and shape" relationships against a person's grain, either. You have to identify each

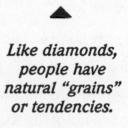

Like diamonds, people have natural "grains" or tendencies.

person's grain and then work with it in order to enhance the relationship.

This is the essence of the Diamond Rule—figuring out each person's natural tendencies and then working with their emotional tendencies, instead of against them, in order to bring out the best in the relationship. To better understand how emotions make up each person's natural "grains" or cleavage points, let's play a quick game.

On a sheet of paper, write a list of 10 things you want most in your life. Now, read back through your list and circle all the answers that are emotions, such as *love… security…* or *freedom.*

The answers you didn't circle are probably things or experiences, such as money, a car, a home, a job, or a specific relationship. Next, complete this statement about all the items you didn't circle above:

"If I had (the item you didn't circle—money, a job, etc.), it would give me (an emotion—freedom, security, happiness, etc.)." For example, "If I had a home it would give me happiness," or "If I had a million dollars, it would give me security," or "If I had a relationship, it would give me love."

My point is this: People are motivated by feelings. When we seek *things,* it's not really the thing that we're after, *but the feeling that the thing gives us!* For example, people will do most anything to get more money. Ironically, it's not the money that people are really after. What they're really after are the *feelings* they think the money will give them. Winning a million dollars in the lottery has actually messed up some people's lives. The money not only didn't give them the positive feelings they thought it would, it gave them pain in the long term!

Question: What are the two best days of boat ownership? Many former boat owners would answer, "The day I bought it, and the day I sold it!" People don't want boats. They buy a boat thinking it will give them the *feeling of excitement or freedom.* Afterward, they discover owning a boat doesn't lead to the feelings they desired, and it's a pain to maintain. Then, they sell it as soon as possible.

What's the difference between a house and a home? It's the feelings of love and happiness that become connected to a particular residence. The best real estate professionals know this, and they make a lot of money selling homes, not houses.

People don't want cars. They want the emotions they believe a particular car will give them. Pontiac isn't selling cars. They're selling excitement! Mercedes and BMW aren't selling cars. They're selling status and prestige. Volvo isn't selling cars. They're selling safety and intelligence. Volvo commercials get people who desperately want to be intelligent, such as people with advanced college degrees, to link Volvo automobiles with the intelligence they desire!

WHY PEOPLE "COME TO MARLBORO COUNTRY"

Unfortunately, cigarette manufacturers understand the power of emotions. They have the Diamond Touch and use it to entice people into buying their products. Take a close look at how they manipulate people's emotions in cigarette commercials. Cigarette companies never sell their product. They know that, in reality, their product has four main attributes: It's highly addictive, it's expensive, it stinks, and it kills people! Trying to push those four product features would be a tough sell in almost any market.

So, cigarette manufacturers don't sell cigarettes. *They sell the emotions people want in their lives,* and they very effectively link one or more of these feelings with their brand of cigarette.

Marlboro has done the best job of selling the emotion instead of the cigarette, and, as a result, is the most popular brand in the United

States and Europe. What emotions do the makers of Marlboro say you will receive when you use their product? Think about the scenes in their ads before you answer. A typical ad has a ruggedly handsome cowboy smoking a cigarette as he relaxes by a campfire. The ad shows only the cowboy, his horse, the beautiful mountains in the background… and the cigarette. The only other image in the ad is a big photo of a pack of Marlboros in the bottom corner. The emotions Marlboro wants you to connect to their product are freedom… virility… individualism… and contentment—four emotions that are highly valued by many people in the Western Hemisphere.

Think about it for a second. How much *logical* sense does it make to believe that becoming addicted to cigarettes will give you more freedom? Zero. Zip. None! But people don't do things for logical reasons. They do things for emotional reasons and sometimes justify their actions with logic. (If people did things for logical reasons, men would be the ones riding side-saddle!) *People do things for emotional reasons. People seek the emotions that make them feel good about themselves.*

▲
People do things for emotional reasons. People seek the emotions that make them feel good about themselves.
▼

RAISIN' THE VALUE OF RAISINS

Let's look at a more positive, yet equally effective, example of how advertising manipulates our emotions. In the 1970s, the California Raisin Growers Association noticed that Americans were eating fewer and fewer raisins. Their advertising campaign couldn't reverse the trend, and sales continued to drop until 1987, when they introduced a totally new ad campaign that re-energized their industry.

Can you remember their advertising campaign before 1987? Most people can't because it was purely logical. It didn't have much impact. Remember the Sun•Maid Lady holding her parasol saying, "There's a drop of sunshine in every raisin. Eat raisins. They're good for you. They're healthy. They'll clean out your colon."

Then in 1987, the Raisin Growers changed their advertising campaign to the Dancing Raisins. Their sales increased dramatically because they stopped trying to sell health and started selling fun! When I present programs to groups, I ask the audience, "How many of you liked watching the Dancing Raisins commercial?" Almost everyone in the room raises their hands. Then I ask them, "What song did they play in the background of the commercial?" Almost everyone answers, "Marvin Gaye's *I Heard It through the Grapevine.*"

Why do those commercials work so well? People watch the Dancing Raisins and feel good. Then one day or one week later they watch the commercial again. They see and hear the Dancing Raisins again and feel good again. After a few repetitions, the good feeling gets connected to the raisins in the nervous systems of the viewers! They become conditioned to want to eat raisins so they can feel good. They buy and eat raisins to get a positive feeling. The commercials are effective and memorable because they are emotional!

So now you've learned the first step to creating close relationships that prosper and last: *When it comes right down to it, people want emotions. When you consistently help people experience the unique emotions they desire, you're living by the Diamond Rule.*

In my opinion, the old saying that "Knowledge is power" is missing a key ingredient. I believe "Knowledge immediately put into action is power!" Take action now by completing the following Exercises for Action and writing your answers in the blank pages at the end of this book. The power and joy of enhanced relationships await you.

EXERCISES FOR ACTION

1. Now that you've read this chapter, try again to think of anything you want in life that doesn't eventually boil down to an emotion. If you come up with an answer that isn't an emotion, repeatedly ask yourself, "If I had that, what feeling would it give me?" I believe you'll see that it always comes down to emotions.

2. Ask a few of your family members, friends, and/or associates at work, "If you could have anything in the world, what would it be?" If the answer isn't an emotion, keep asking, "If you had that, what feeling would it give you?" Again, I believe you'll notice that what people really want are emotions.

3. For one week, analyze all the television and print ads you see. What emotions are the advertisers trying to connect to their products?

In this chapter, you've learned the first key to giving people what they really want. Key #1 is: When it comes right down to it, people want positive emotions in their lives. In the next chapter, you'll learn that "not all emotions are created equal."

Read on to discover why... **Values Are the "What."**

CHAPTER 4

Your Values Are the "What"

◇

The trouble with people is twofold.
They cannot learn truths that are too complicated;
and they forget truths that are too simple.
—Rebecca West

ake a moment to think about each of the following key emotions:

1. LOVE
2. SECURITY
3. ADVENTURE
4. SUCCESS
5. FREEDOM

It's fair to say that one or more of these five emotions motivate almost everything you do in your life. Why? Because we humans are emotional beings. Once we're assured that our basic *physical needs*, i.e., food and shelter have been satisfied, then we start *looking to satisfy our emotional needs*—love... security... adventure... success... freedom.

I could have listed hundreds of emotions, but I reduced the list to the five key emotions that drive most people in our culture. Now, take a look at the five key emotions again.

____ LOVE

____ SECURITY

____ ADVENTURE

____ SUCCESS

____ FREEDOM

To determine which emotions have the most impact on the decisions you make in your life, write a number from 1 to 5 in the blank next to each emotion, 1 being the most important emotion in your life, and 5 being the least important emotion. (If you have difficulty deciding between two emotions, ask yourself this question: "If I could only have one of these two emotions, which would I choose?")

The emotion you selected first is the one you value the most in your life. It's the emotion that's most important for you to experience. As a result, all of the major decisions in your life—who you marry... where you live... what you buy... how you spend your leisure time— will be dominated by this emotion.

As you might imagine, not everyone would order the emotions the way you did. People value emotions differently. This variety is what makes the world an interesting and challenging place in which to live. To practice the Diamond Rule—which means giving people what they *really want* in all the relationships of your life—you must understand their unique set of Values.

VALUES EQUAL OUR STRONGEST EMOTIONS

Let's take a moment to discuss Values and how they relate to our emotions. I use the word Values to describe the emotions that people desire the most. The reason is simple. Emotions are what motivate us. Emotions are the feelings we seek most in life, so it stands to reason that our strongest emotions will dictate our key Values and vice versa.

For example, if freedom is an emotion that you seek in life, then you'll value the things, people, and experiences that trigger the feeling of freedom. That's why I equate Values with our strongest emotions— they're really one and the same.

Values or key emotions are *what* people want to experience most in their lives. That's why I say Values are the WHAT.

> ▲
> *Values or emotions are what people want to experience most in their lives. That's why I say Values are the WHAT.*
> ▼

VALUES ARE THE FEELINGS PEOPLE MOST WANT TO EXPERIENCE

Let me share a personal example of Values in action. At one time in my life, I was a very successful dentist. I had a huge dental practice and was making tons of money. But I absolutely hated being tied down to the "drilling, filling, and billing" of dentistry. So I sold my practice and got completely out of the profession.

Today, as a speaker and author, I choose the projects I want to work on and travel the world sharing ideas I believe in. Our house is on the top of a hill. We can see 25 miles into the distance from our back yard. For recreation, I frequently go scuba diving or do some other outdoor activity, such as skiing, tennis, or golf.

From this small slice of my life, I'll bet you can figure out which of the five emotions I value most in life. *Freedom is at the top of my list!* When I have freedom, I have the space to love others, be successful, and have adventure in my life. I'm attracted to jobs that give me freedom, sports that provide freedom, and other people who value freedom.

My wife, Dawn, also puts freedom at the top of her list, too. Many times during the year I'll leave town for more than a week. Does Dawn cuddle up to me as I'm walking out the door and whisper gently in my ear, "I really wish you didn't have to go"? Heck no! She says, "See ya! Don't call home 'cause I probably won't be here!" Our relationship works well because we share freedom as the #1 value in our lives.

If you're thinking that some other emotion other than freedom should be #1 in our lives, that just means that you have a different set of Values concerning what a "good" marriage should be. This is natural—we all have a tendency to believe that "My Values are the right Values!" But you must remind yourself that the Diamond Rule means you agree to treat each person as they uniquely want to be treated, not as you and your dominant Values think that person should be treated.

THE IMPORTANCE OF KNOWING SOMEONE'S VALUES

Here's an example of the potential danger of not knowing someone's Values. Occasionally, I'll talk to a financial planner who is trying to sell me an investment plan. What emotion do you think he tries to sell me nine times out of ten? *Security!* It's truly amazing and amusing to see the sales process unfold. In the beginning of the sales call, the planner will ask me, "At what age do you want to retire?" I answer, "Retire from what? I never want to retire. I'm having way too much fun to retire!"

You should see the look on his face. He doesn't know what to do! My response completely messes up his sales presentation because he can't pull out his handy-dandy little chart that shows how much money I need put away each year to comfortably retire at age 65.

Then he will say something that sounds to me like, "Well, don't you want to build a nest egg so you can retire in Yuma, Arizona, to an old person depository and play shuffleboard every afternoon and bingo on Wednesday evenings?" That vision of the future makes me sick. I want to keep "working" until I drop. I want to keep working until eventually I have a fantastic place in the mountains where my family and I can ski, hike, bike, and enjoy all the freedom the world has to offer. If a financial planner would sell me a plan that would give me freedom, I'd be all ears.

When I do the LOVE, SECURITY, ADVENTURE, SUCCESS, FREEDOM exercise with a room full of people, each emotion is selected as #1 by at least 10% of the room. When I'm in a room full of salespeople, success and freedom are selected most often. When I'm in a room full of social workers, love is the #1 choice. This is another indication that people have different Values and tend to choose careers that give them their highest Values.

I had an interesting and enlightening experience when doing this exercise in Malaysia in 1994. Most of the people in the room couldn't choose a highest Value from my usual list of LOVE, SECURITY, ADVENTURE, SUCCESS, and FREEDOM. I could see from their facial expressions they were in real pain trying to make a decision. Finally, they told me, "We don't want most of the emotions on your list!"

With their input, I changed the list to:
CHARM
GRACE
LOVE
TRANSCENDENCE
PEACE
Different cultures often have different Values. To truly understand a culture, you must understand its Values! Likewise, to truly understand people and give them what they really want, you must know their unique set of Values.

Let's review what you've learned so far:

1. When it comes right down to it, people want emotions.

2. Values are the emotions people want most.

3. Each person has a unique set of Values.

4. In order to give people what they really want, you must discover their Values.

HOW TO DISCOVER A PERSON'S VALUES

There are two ways to discover a person's Values. The best way is to watch people and listen to what they say. Observing people with your antennae up will tell you what people value the most in their lives.

The second way to discover a person's Values is to ask. You'll be amazed at what people will tell if you have a moderate level of rapport with them and ask the right questions in the right way.

To be an effective Values detective, follow these five steps:

1. Establish some rapport with the person. Be friendly and caring. If you've just met the person, engage in small talk to break the ice. Ask about things that interest that person.

2. Let the person know why you're asking these questions. If you want to explore a co-worker's Values, say something like, "Mary, I really want to know the people I work with because everyone is different and everyone has different wants and needs. Tell me... " (then go to the Values Question given in Step 3).

3. Ask the Values Question: *"What's most important to you in* (the Values area you want to explore)*?"* The exact question you ask will be determined by your relationship with the person and the Values area you want to explore. For example, if you want to discover someone's Life Values, you would ask, *"What's most important to you in life?"* If you're a mother and you want to discover your son's Values in his relationship with you, you would ask, *"What's most important to you in a relationship with a mom?"* If you have a key associate at work, it would be valuable to ask the question, *"What's most important to you in a relationship with an associate?"* In Chapters 6 through 9, you'll learn the precise Values Questions you need to ask in the most important relationships of your life.

4. If you want to discover a second Value for a particular Values area, ask, *"What else is important to you in* (the Values area you want to explore)*?"* For example, *"What else is important to you in a relationship with an associate?"* The number of Values you discover depends on the depth of your relationship and the amount of time you have with the person.

5. If you elicit more than one Value, make sure you put them in order by asking, "If you could have only one of these emotions, which one would you choose?" And then ask this

question of each of the remaining Values until the entire list is in order from most important (#1) to least important.

Now it's time to apply the information in this chapter to your life by completing the Exercises for Action below. Please do them now before you read on.

Exercises for Action

1. Think of a poor relationship you've had in the past. As you might expect, the person probably had a different set of Values than you. In the blank pages in the back of this book, record what you think the difference was.

2. If you currently have a relationship with a person from a different culture, how do the Values of that culture differ from our culture's Values? Record your answer in the back of this book.

Values are the "What" people want in their lives. The subject of the next chapter is Sparks. Sparks are the things that have to happen for people to experience their Values. *If Values are WHAT people want, Sparks are HOW they want it.*

Intrigued? Read on to discover why—Sparks are the "HOW."

CHAPTER 5

Sparks Are the "How"

*The real voyage of discovery consists not
in seeking new landscapes but in
having new eyes.*
—Marcel Proust

hen I was growing up, the kids in the neighborhood
would get together to play almost every day during
summer vacation. We'd play baseball and tag during the
day and Hide-and-Seek in the evenings.

But no matter what game we played, we'd spend at least half the
time bickering over the rules. One person would be playing under

one set of rules, while someone on the other team would be operating under a different set of rules. All of the participants would be confused because someone didn't know the "rules of the game" (i.e., *your* rules!). To keep the game going, we had to reach an agreement on the rules in question. But in the process, there was a lot of confusion. A lot of misunderstandings. A lot of arguments. A lot of accusations of "cheating." And a lot of anger.

The same thing happens in real life. Let's say you're in an important relationship with a person. Even if you have a common set of Values, each of you has a set of rules concerning the relationship and how it "should" work. Because people are different, the two sets of rules are probably different. Unless you get clear on the rules, there will be conflict.

▲

Sparks are the things that have to happen for people to experience their Values.

▼

In this book, the word we will use for rules is "Sparks." Sparks are the things that have to happen for people to experience their Values. Just as a spark is necessary to start a fire, a Spark is something that must happen in order for someone to "light the fire" of their Value.

Each person's Sparks for their Values are unique. And just like a game of baseball or tag or Hide-and-Seek, this unique set of rules determines how a person wants to play the relationship "game" with you.

Sparks Are the Things That Have to Happen for People to Experience Their Values

Giving people what they really want in life is more than just avoiding conflict. It's pro-actively discovering what people want (their Values) and how they want it (their Sparks). Once you discover someone's Sparks, you can give them what they want in the way they want it on a consistent basis.

Here's an example of Values and Sparks in action. Love is a Value that is high on most people's Values lists. It is for my wife, Dawn, and me. If you've ever been in love, you know that different people have different Sparks for what has to happen for them to feel love. In our relationship, I could never tell Dawn I love her, and it wouldn't bother her one bit! It's not one of her Sparks for love. She feels love when we go places and do things together—when we share experiences.

If you're shaking your head in amazement, it just means that you have different Sparks for love than Dawn. If you're nodding in approval right now, it means that you have the same Spark for love as Dawn. I want my wife to feel loved. So, what do I do on a regular basis? I plan trips where we go places and do things together.

Speaking of the different Sparks people have for love, I once did a program for a large audience. I had them do the LOVE, SECURITY, ADVENTURE, SUCCESS, FREEDOM exercise you did in Chapter 4.

As I read the five Values one at a time, I had the people in the audience raise their hands if they had that Value as their #1 choice. There were two women sitting next to each other who both raised their hands when I said "Love."

It was obvious that the older of the two women was in a lot of pain. Deep frown lines creased her face. Her posture was rigid. Obviously, she wasn't getting much love in her life. Hoping I could help her break through her pain, I asked, "What has to happen for you to experience love in your life?"

She paused, then answered, "I'll feel loved when I'm married to this one man."

"Who's the guy?" I asked innocently.

"My ex-husband," she replied solemnly.

Talk about opening a can of worms! I found out later that the woman's husband had left her for another woman. She was still attached to the guy, but he had moved on. The woman's highest Value was love. Her Spark for love was being married to an ex-husband who wanted nothing to do with her. This woman had set up her life so that she couldn't win. It's sad, isn't it? Yet at one time or another, we've all wished for a Spark that couldn't be delivered. Incidentally, I talked to the woman in private after the program and showed her how her Spark for love was leading to unhappiness and suggested some other Sparks that would help her feel love on a daily basis.

The second woman also raised her hand when I said "Love." As I looked at her, I saw that she had a high degree of love and positive energy radiating from her body. I immediately knew she was getting a lot of love in her life. To confirm my assumption, I asked her the same question as the first woman:

"What has to happen for you to experience love in your life?"

She said, "I feel love whenever anyone smiles at me, does anything for me, or talks to me in a kind way. I feel love when I'm with my family, friends, or people here at work. I feel love whenever I smile at people, talk to them, or help them in any way." You could hear the whole room saying, "Ohhh!" The contrast between the two women's rules for the Love Game was striking.

The second woman's Spark for experiencing love was so all-inclusive that she felt the emotion frequently. She set up her game of life so she could win on a regular basis. Both of these women had the same #1 Value—Love. However, they had two vastly different sets of Sparks for what had to happen for them to experience love. The first woman's Spark led to an absence of love. The second woman's Sparks led to an abundance of love.

HOW SPARKS SAVED A DOOMED LIMOUSINE SERVICE

Here's a different example of the power of understanding other people's Values and Sparks. About five years ago I did a sales training program for a group of 300 people from a wide variety of organizations. After the program was over, a man came up to me and said, "I need some help. I own a limousine service that's about to go broke. I've cut my prices as far as I can, and people still don't use my services. They call me on the phone and the first question they ask is, 'How much?' I tell them my fee schedule. Then I say, 'We have some excellent limousines staffed by courteous drivers.' About one out of ten potential customers calls me back."

I said, "I know why you're having so much trouble. You're not discovering people's Values and Sparks. There's no way that you can make the sale and then give them the service they desire unless you find out what people want and how they want it."

I suggested that the next time a customer called, he ask the key questions that would reveal the person's Values and Sparks:

Question 1: "What is most important to you during your limo ride?"

Question 2: What has to happen for you to feel _____?"

The man was desperate, so I knew he would follow through.

A month later, I got a call from the guy.

He was beside himself with excitement.

"Nate, I can hardly believe it! I'm selling eight out of ten people who call me now, and I've raised my prices 15%!"

"I'm not surprised," I said. "You're asking those questions I gave you, aren't you?"

"I sure am!"

"You're finally discovering what people really want and how they want it, aren't you?" I said.

"You bet!" he replied.

He then told me the following story that illustrated the power of his newfound skill. "Two Mondays ago a woman called me and said she wanted a limo for Friday evening. Her first question was, 'How much?' I told her, 'We have several different plans depending on what you want from the evening. But first, would you mind answering a couple of questions? I really want to get to know the people I serve because everyone has different wants and needs.'

"'Sure,' she said. "Then I asked her the first question you taught me: 'What's most important to you in your limousine ride on Friday evening?' She answered, 'Well, five of my lady friends and I are going out on the town, and we want a wild, crazy, outrageous evening!'

"I wrote down wild, crazy, outrageous evening on a piece of paper as her #1 Value for the limo ride.

"Then I asked her the second question you taught me. I said, 'That's great! Now, what has to happen in order for you to have that wild, crazy, outrageous evening?' She answered, 'You know what? We want a moon roof in the limo so all six of us can stick our heads through the roof and yell at the guys on the sidewalk.'

"On my sheet of paper, I wrote down Spark #1—moon roof.

"Then I asked her another question: 'What else has to happen for you to have a wild, crazy, outrageous evening this Friday?' She answered, 'Well, we want to have some champagne in the limo.'

"I remembered what you told me, Nate, about how I had to be specific with a person's Sparks, so I asked her what kind of champagne she wanted. She said, 'Korbel champagne.' I asked, 'Do you want Green Label or White Label Korbel?' She answered, 'The Green Label.' Then I asked, 'How many bottles do you want?' She said, 'Three bottles.'

"I wrote down on my piece of paper Spark #2—three bottles of Green Label Korbel champagne.

"Things were going so well I decided to go for her third Spark. I asked her, 'What else would we have to do for you to have a wild, crazy, outrageous evening this Friday?' She enthusiastically answered, 'We want to have a guy driver. We want him to be young and outgoing. We want someone we can really talk to and who will talk to us. Ya know what? We want a hunk!'

"I wrote down Spark #3—hunky male driver."

Do you see what's happening here? My friend is learning exactly what his client wants and how she wants it. He's being precise in his discovery of her Values and Sparks. Remember what he used to say to all his prospects? "We have some excellent limos staffed by courteous drivers." One big problem—the woman didn't want an excellent limo staffed by a courteous driver. She wanted a moon-roofed limo loaded with three bottles of chilled Green Label Korbel champagne and chauffeured by a young, outgoing, good-looking male driver!

Armed with this information, how difficult was it for the guy to make the sale? Extremely easy! Here's what he told his client to close the deal:

"This Friday you and your guests will have our finest limousine, Silver Cloud #7. It has a double moon roof so up to eight people can stand up and yell at the guys on the sidewalk. I'll have three bottles of chilled Green Label Korbel champagne waiting for you, and do you know who your driver will be? Crazy Larry. He's young, outgoing— "a real hunk," as you put it. You'll have a wild, crazy, outrageous time with him!"

My friend quoted her a price that was 15% higher than the competition. Do you think he got the job? Sure. Why? Because he showed her how she could get exactly what she wanted in the way she wanted it with his limousine service. Then on Friday night, he gave her the service he promised. After he did that, do you think she will use his service again? Absolutely. Do you think she will refer her friends to him? Positively.

This is just one story, but it exemplifies the power in discovering people's Values and Sparks in all the relationships of your life. In the last chapter you learned the Values Questions to discover what people want.

Now it's time to learn the Sparks Questions to discover how they want it.

DISCOVERING A PERSON'S SPARKS

1. After you learn the person's first Value with the Values Question, discover one or more of their Sparks for that particular Value. After you have done that, you can discover Value #2 and the Sparks for that Value.

2. Ask the Sparks Question, *"What has to happen in order for you to feel* (the Value you just learned)?" In the limousine example, the Sparks Question was, "What has to happen for you to have a wild, crazy, outrageous evening this Friday?" The first Spark discovered was, "A moon roof."

3. There may be multiple Sparks for each Value. To discover these additional Sparks, ask the question, *"What else has to happen in order for you to feel* (the Value you just learned)?" The Sparks Question can be worded differently depending on the situation. In the limousine story, for example, the second Sparks Question was, "What else has to happen for you to have a wild, crazy, outrageous evening this Friday?" Her second Spark was, "Three bottles of Green Label Korbel champagne." Her third Spark was, "A hunky young driver."

As you will see in the coming chapters, there are many ways to word the Values and Sparks Questions. The exact wording isn't as important as making the Diamond Rule a guiding principle in all your relationships. Living a life based on discovering what people want— and how they want it—and then giving it to them when it's in their best long-term interest will also bring you the emotions you desire and deserve.

Have you ever had a relationship with someone that ended on a sour note, and you didn't know what happened? You now have the tools to revisit that relationship to discover exactly why it ended. That's what you will do in this chapter's Exercises for Action.

Do them now while the information is fresh in your mind.

EXERCISES FOR ACTION

1. Think of a business relationship you've had that was basically good but which went through a difficult time or ended because you broke one of the other person's "rules." What was the rule you broke? What upset did that create? How did you resolve the upset (i.e., did you get clear on the rules of the game)? Record your answers in the back of this book.

2. Think of a personal relationship you've had that was basically a good one but which went downhill because you broke one of the other person's rules. What was the rule you broke? What upset did that create? How did you resolve the upset (i.e., did you get clear on the rules of the game)? Record your answers in the back of this book.

Now that you know the power of discovering people's Values and Sparks, it's time to start applying your knowledge to the relationships in your life. Let's move on to Section Three and begin **Applying the Diamond Rule to Your "Crown Jewels."**

Section 3

Applying the Diamond Rule to Your "Crown Jewels"

Section 3

Applying the Diamond Rule to Your "Crown Jewels"

Let's Review:

1 When it comes right down to it, people want emotions.

2 Values are the emotions people want most.

3. Each person has a unique set of Values.

4. In order to give people what they really want, you must discover their Values.

5. Sparks are what have to happen for people to experience their Values. Each person has a unique set of Sparks for each of their Values.

What's Ahead:

In this Section, you'll learn the Values and Sparks Discovery Process, that is, the specific questions you need to ask to discover a person's unique set of Values and Sparks in four different kinds of relationships:

1. Husband/wife

2. Parent/child

3. Friendships

4. Co-workers

With the Values and Sparks Discovery Process, you can learn a tremendous amount about WHAT people want and HOW they want it in a relatively short period of time.

CHAPTER 6

Husband/Wife Relationships

◇

*You get married not to be happy
but to make each other happy.*
—Roy L. Smith
Author & Motivator

've purposely put the Husband/Wife Relationships chapter first in this section because it's the most important relationship in most people's lives. In my opinion, more marriages and other intimate relationships have ended because:

1. One or both people in the relationship didn't accurately discover the other person's Values and Sparks, and then...

2. One or both people in the relationship didn't consistently give the other person what they wanted in the way they wanted it (when it was in the other person's best long-term interest).

I know this may sound simplistic, but it's true. Just take a few moments to reflect on your own life. Think of an important relationship in your life that ended with an upset. What Value(s) and Spark(s) of *yours* were broken? What Value(s) and Spark(s) of the *other person* were broken? Do you see how a failure to understand a person's Values and a failure to give them the Sparks they want contributed to the deterioration of the relationship?

Now answer this vitally important question: How might things have been different if both of you had accurately discovered the other person's Values and Sparks and then given the other person what they wanted in the way they wanted it (when it was in their best long-term interest)?

Now can you see why the Diamond Rule is such a profound principle? Once you fully understand how to identify Values and how to deliver Sparks, then you have the power to transform your relationships and take them to a whole new level of value and intimacy!

THE VALUES AND SPARKS DISCOVERY PROCESS FOR A MARRIAGE

You've learned the theory of the Diamond Rule—to treat others as they *uniquely* want to be treated. Now it's time to put the theory into practice in your own life. Let's start by learning the questions and strategies that will reveal the Values and Sparks of your husband, wife, or significant other.

A. Explore the Relationship Values Area

First, take a moment to explain to your spouse why you want to ask the following questions. Explain that the more you understand your spouse's Values and what to do and say to deliver those Values, the better your relationship will be. Then begin your questioning. I suggest you write the answers down for future reference.

1. Start by asking the Values Question, *"What's most important to you in a relationship with a husband/wife?"* Discover the #1 Value for this area.

2. For the Value you discovered in Step 1 above, ask the Sparks Question, *"What has to happen in order for you to feel (#1 Value)?"* Discover the first Spark for the #1 Value.

3. Discover at least two other Sparks for the #1 Value by asking, *"What else has to happen in order for you to feel (#1 Value)?"*

4. Discover at least two other Values for the Relationship Values area by asking, *"What else is important to you in a relationship with a husband/wife?"* Then repeat Steps 2 and 3 to discover at least two Sparks for each additional Value you discover.

B. Explore the Life Values Area

1. Ask the Values Question, *"What's most important to you in life?"* Discover the #1 Value for this area.

2. For the Value you discovered in step 1 above, ask the Sparks Question, *"What has to happen in order for you to feel (#1 Value)?"* Discover the first Spark for the #1 Value.

3. Discover at least two other Sparks for his/her #1 Value by asking, *"What else has to happen in order for you to feel (#1 Value)?"*

4. Discover at least two other Values from the Life Values area by asking, *"What else is important to you in life?"* Then repeat steps 2 and 3 to discover at least two Sparks for each additional Value you discover.

When you use the Values and Sparks Discovery Process with

▲

When you use the Values and Sparks Discovery Process with your spouse, be prepared to learn more about them in one hour than you have over the course of your entire relationship.

▼

your spouse, be prepared to learn more about them in one hour than you have over the course of your entire relationship. Be prepared to gain the information you will need to make a dramatic, consistent, and long-lasting improvement in the quality of the relationship!

Remember: A Value is always an emotion. A Spark is something that has to happen for the person to feel the emotion.

ADDITIONAL INSIGHTS

We're all painfully aware that life doesn't unfold as neatly as a TV sitcom. Which in this case means that you may get a Sparks answer when you ask a Values Question, and vice versa. As with any new skill, it will take a little time before you master the Values and Sparks Process.

Also, be certain you approach the Values and Sparks Process from a position of giving. You're learning information about your spouse so that you can do a better job of giving them what they want in the way they want it.

You are also giving them the gift of self-understanding. This may be the first time they have consciously examined their Values and Sparks in a relationship—which is valuable in and of itself. After you discover their Values and Sparks, they may volunteer to reverse roles, or it may be appropriate for you to ask them to elicit your Values and Sparks, as well.

Here are some tips that will help you stay on track and get the most out of the Process:

1. If the person gives you a Spark when you ask the Values Question, just say, *"That's great! If you had* (the Spark they gave you), *what would that mean to you? What would that give you?"* Remember, a Value is always an emotion. A Spark is something that has to happen for the person to feel the emotion.

2. If the person is giving you a series of Sparks when you're asking the Values Question, you may have to mentally analyze the Sparks and suggest a Value. You may want to say something like this: *"It sounds like* (the Value you believe the person is referring to) *is very important to you."* For example, if someone says, "You have to listen to me and not contradict me in front of other people," your response might be, "It sounds like respect is important to you. Is that right?" The person will verbally and nonverbally tell you if you guessed right. If you're wrong, guess again.

3. If you ask a question, and the person says, "I don't know," don't let them off the hook. They do know. The person probably just hasn't thought about it in a while. Just come back with, *"I know you don't know, but if you did know, what would the answer be?"* Or, *"I know it may be hard to think right now, but just give me something off the top of your head."* Be politely persistent.

4. If the person has trouble coming up with a Spark for a specific Value, have them remember a specific time when they deeply felt the Value. What was happening in the moment that sparked them to feel the emotion? For example, if the Value you discovered for your spouse was love, and they're having trouble coming up with a Spark, ask, *"Can you remember a time when you felt deeply loved? What was happening that sparked the feeling of love?"*

5. Be sure that each Spark is worded in a positive way. If the person words the Spark in a negative way, clarify what the positive would be. As an example, if your spouse says, "I feel loved when you don't ignore me at parties," you can respond, "Good! What can I do at parties so that I can enjoy myself and still show you I love you?"

6. Be certain that the person is very specific on their Sparks. Remember my friend with the limousine company. It was much better for him to discover that the woman wanted "three bottles of Green Label Korbel champagne" rather than "some champagne." The Spark should be specific enough that you know exactly what you can do to give the person what they want.

7. Occasionally, you may want to word a Sparks Question in a way that focuses the person's attention on what you can do to give them their Values. For example, if the person says they want love in their life, you can ask, *"What do I do now, or what could I do in the future, that would make you feel the most love?"*

8. The number of Values and Sparks you discover depends on the depth of your relationship and the amount of time you have spent with the person. Lots of depth and time (i.e., in most intimate relationships) equals many Values and Sparks. Little depth and time (i.e., with an occasional customer at your business) equals few Values and Sparks.

9. You can word the Values and Sparks Questions differently depending on the situation and the kinds of answers the person is giving you. You can see this in the examples I've used in this and subsequent chapters. The Values and Sparks Discovery Process is much more than a series of specific questions. <u>It's a consistent way of thinking that can be summed up as, "What do they want (their Values), and how do they want it (their Sparks)?"</u>

10. Before you begin, get permission to write down people's answers. This will provide you with a written record and make the process even more important to them.

11. As you go through the Values and Sparks Discovery Process, do not be judgmental! Making sarcastic remarks or editorializing while someone is opening up to you is a surefire way to end the discussion, once and for all! Just because you discover a person's Values and Sparks does not mean that you agree with them, or that you are planning on giving the person exactly what they want. Depending on the nature of the relationship, you may have to negotiate "the rules of the game;" or, in relationships where one of the "players" is young or inexperienced, (e.g., parent/child), you may have to educate and guide them during the process. In Chapter 10, *Creative Giving,* you will learn how to educate people, as well as what to do if you believe the Values and/or Sparks are not in the person's best long-term interest.

12. If the person is resistant to the Values and Sparks Process, you need to gain more of their trust. Be sure they understand why you want the information, and/or proceed again at a more convenient time.

13. People's Values and Sparks change over time. Be sure to check in with the people in your close relationships at regular intervals.

14. In certain situations, it may be best to do the Values and Sparks Discovery Process with some lightness and humor. Make the process enjoyable, not like the police are interrogating a suspect in an old "cops and robbers" movie.

An Example of the Husband/Wife Values Discovery Process

Wife   "Honey, I really want to make our relationship even better than it already is. To do that, I need to learn more precisely what you want in our relationship and in life. After I'm done, you can ask me the same questions if you'd like."

Husband   "Sounds like you've been watching Oprah again."

Wife   "Actually, I've been reading this book. Do you want to take a look?"

Husband   "That's okay. Ask away."

Wife   "I like to start with the easy questions. When it comes right down to it, what's most important to you in a relationship with a wife?" (The Values Question to discover his #1 Relationship Value)

Husband "Oh, I don't know. A lot of things." (Typical unspecific "guy" answer)

Wife "Of all those 'things' on your list, which would be most important?" (A question that elegantly guides him to be specific)

Husband "Well, I guess being respected." (His #1 Relationship Value)

Wife "Great! What do I do right now, or what could I do, to make you feel respected?" (A form of the Sparks Question)

Husband "I don't know."

Wife "I know it's kind of hard to think of something right now, but just give me something off the top of your head." (She's wisely not taking "I don't know" for an answer.)

Husband "Boy, I really can't think of anything."

Wife "Can you remember a time when you really felt respected by me?" (She directs his focus to the past.)

Husband "Well, yeah."

Wife "When was that, and what did I do that gave you the feeling?"

Husband "It was the time when I got my first promotion at work. You hugged me and told me how proud you were of me!" (She finally gets his #1 Spark for the Value of respect. Now, she has one way to show him respect. She can obtain more by asking the following question.)

Wife "That's great, honey. What else has to happen for you to feel respect? What's another way you feel truly respected?" (A Sparks Question for the respect Value)

Husband "You're persistent, aren't you? Well, I feel respected when you don't criticize me." (Have you ever had a conversation in your marriage that started like this? Now is the time to get some resolution on how you can communicate your desires while your spouse maintains respect.)

Wife "What can I do when I don't like something you've done, so I can get my point across and you can feel respected?" (She's turning his negative "Don't criticize me" into a positive "What can I do?... " and discovering a way in which both of their desires can be met.)

Husband "You can say you don't like what I just did without making me seem like I was wrong. You can ask me not to do something instead of demanding that I don't do it."

Wife "That sounds fair enough. Will you remind me if I fall back into my old routine?"

Husband "Sure!" (He's liking the process better already!)

The wife would now discover more Sparks for the Value of respect. Then she would discover more Values and Sparks in the area of a husband/wife relationship. Now she can move on to the Life Values area.

       Wife "Here's another easy question. What's most important to you in life?"

Husband "Doing well at work." (She asks a Values Question, but he answers with a Spark.)

       Wife "If you did well at work, what would that mean to you?"

Husband "It would mean that I would be moving ahead." (He gives her another Spark.)

       Wife "If you were moving ahead, what would that mean to you?"

Husband "It would mean that I might get a promotion." (He gives her a third Spark.)

       Wife "It sounds to me like being successful is very important to you?" (She doesn't want to continue chasing Sparks and suggests the Value of success.)

Husband "You're right. Success is very important to me." (Hooray! She guessed correctly.)

       Wife "One of the things you mentioned that had to happen for you to have success was that you had to do well at work. Can you be more specific?"

Husband   "I do well at work when I feel good about the quality of my work." (His first Spark for success)

Wife   "What can I do to help you move ahead at work, feel good about your work, and be more successful?"

Husband   "Every once in a while, I need to bring work home. When I do, I need to go into my cave and be left alone for a couple of hours."

Wife   "The family and I can do that as long as it doesn't happen more than once a week. Is that fair?" (She's negotiating a Spark that will work for everyone involved.)

Husband   "Sure."

Wife   "What else has to happen for you to feel success in your life?" (She's after his second Spark for success.)

Husband   "I feel successful when I'm recognized for my achievements." (His second Spark for success is being recognized.)

Wife   "Specifically, how do you like to be recognized?" (She wants some clarity so she knows exactly what she can do.)

Husband   "Awards are nice, but verbal congratulations are better."

Wife   "What else has to happen for you to feel success in your life?" (She's on a roll now!)

Husband   "I'll feel successful when we can put away $10,000 a year for retirement." (His third Spark for success in his life is putting $10,000 a year into a retirement account.)

The wife can now discover more Sparks for the Life Value of success. Then she can discover more Values and the Sparks that go with them in the Life Values area. As you may have noticed, she told him a couple of ways she can give him what he wants in life in the way he wants it. At the end of the conversation, she can look over her notes and see many other ways that she can be a caring Values and Sparks provider.

As you might imagine, the Exercises for Action section is especially comprehensive for this chapter, and it's extremely important that you complete it this week. You now have a nugget of knowledge. Turn that knowledge into power by doing the Exercises for Action with your spouse or significant other tonight.

EXERCISES FOR ACTION

The Values and Sparks Discovery Process for a Marriage

First, explain to your partner why you want to ask these questions. Of course, the best way to do this is to study this book together. Record all of your answers in the back of this book.

A. Explore the Relationship Values Area

1. Ask the Values Question, *"What's most important to you in a relationship with a husband/wife?"* Discover the #1 Value for this area.

2. For the Value you discovered in Step 1 above, ask the Sparks Question, *"What has to happen in order for you to feel (#1 Value)?"* Discover the first Spark for the #1 Value.

3. Discover at least two other Sparks for the #1 Value by asking, *"What else has to happen in order for you to feel (#1 Value)?"*

4. Discover at least two other Values for the Relationship Values area by asking, *"What else is important to you in a relationship with a husband/wife?"* Then repeat Steps 2 and 3 to discover at least two Sparks for each additional Value you discover.

B. Explore the Life Values Area

1. Ask the Values Question, *"What's most important to you in life?"* Discover the #1 Value for this area.

2. For the Value you discovered in Step 1 above, ask the Sparks Question, *"What has to happen in order for you to feel (#1 Value)?"* Discover the first Spark for the #1 Value.

3. Discover at least two other Sparks for the #1 Value by asking, *"What else has to happen in order for you to feel (#1 Value)?"*

4. Discover at least two other Values for the Life Values area by asking, *"What else is important to you in life?"* Then repeat Steps 2 and 3 to discover at least two Sparks for each additional Value you discover.

In this chapter, you learned the Values and Sparks Discovery Process for Husband/Wife relationships. In the next chapter, you will move on to another important relationship—the Parent/Child relationship.

A word of warning—Parent/Child relationships can be especially challenging for two reasons:

1. You have two unique people with different Values and Sparks.

2. The two people are from different generations. Generations have different sets of Values and Sparks that are reinforced by the members of that generation. This is usually referred to as the "Generation Gap" and will test your ability to be non-judgmental!

I know that you're up to the challenge. After you complete this chapter's Exercises for Action, read on to discover how you can improve your... **Parent/Child Relationships.**

CHAPTER 7

Parent/Child Relationships

◇

.What kids really need is a good listening to.
—Anonymous

y good friend Becky believed in the Diamond Rule and practiced the Diamond Touch in all of her relationships, even the relationship with her five-year-old son, Josh. Becky was prepared to ask Josh the right questions. But she had to admit that Josh's quirky answer threw her for a loop.

"What's most important to you in a relationship with a mom?" Becky asked.

"Love," Josh answered.

"That's great, Josh. I really want you to feel loved. What can I do to make you feel the most loved?" Becky asked.

Josh pondered for a moment before blurting, "Tickle my toes when you tuck me in bed at night."

Becky knew that Josh liked having his toes tickled, but she never knew it was that important to him. So what did she do on a regular basis to make him feel more loved? Tickled his toes when she tucked him in bed at night.

▲

We're all "wired" differently when it comes to the pleasure we desire and how we want that pleasure delivered.

▼

I'll be the first to admit that having my toes tickled isn't my #1 Spark for love. But that's what makes life so interesting and challenging. We're all "wired" differently when it comes to the pleasure we desire and how we want that pleasure delivered. The Values and Sparks Discovery Process is the best method I know to learn the "wiring plan" of the people with whom we have relationships.

Sometimes it seems to adults that children are "wired" in an incomprehensible fashion. That's why it's especially important for you to do the following Values and Sparks Discovery Process with your children.

THE VALUES AND SPARKS DISCOVERY PROCESS FOR A PARENT/CHILD RELATIONSHIP

First, explain to your child why you want to ask these questions. Let them know that you love them and want to get to know them better.

A. Explore the Relationship Values Area

1. Ask this Values Question: *"What's most important to you in a relationship with a mom/dad?"* Discover your child's #1 Value for this area.

2. For the Value you discovered in Step 1, ask the Sparks Question, *"What has to happen in order for you to feel (#1 Value)?"* Discover the first Spark for the #1 Value.

3. Discover at least two other Sparks for the #1 Value by asking, *"What else has to happen in order for you to feel (#1 Value)?"*

4. Discover three other Values for the Relationship Values area by asking, *"What else is important to you in a relationship with a mom/dad?"* Then repeat Steps 2 and 3 to discover at least two Sparks for each additional Value you discover.

B. Explore the Life Values Area

1. Ask this Values Question: *"What's most important to you in life?"* Discover your child's #1 Value for this area.

2. For the Value you discovered in Step 1 above, ask the Sparks Question, *"What has to happen in order for you to feel (#1 Value)?"* Discover the first Spark for the #1 Value.

3. Discover at least two other Sparks for the #1 Value by asking, *"What else has to happen in order for you to feel (#1 Value)?"*

4. Discover at least two other Values for the Life Values area by asking, *"What else is important to you in life?"* Then repeat Steps 2 and 3 to discover at least two Sparks for each additional Value you discover.

An Example Using the Values Discovery Process in a Parent/Child Relationship

I have a wonderful teenage daughter, Belinda. About four years ago, I did the Values Discovery Process with her. Here's an edited version of how it went.

Nate   "Belinda, I want to be the best possible dad I can. In order for me to do that, I'd like to know what's really important to you. This is the same kind of thing we talked about a year ago. Is it okay if I ask you those questions again?"

Belinda   "Sure, Dad."

Nate   "What's most important to you in a relationship with a dad?" (The Values Question to discover her #1 Value)

Belinda "Oh, probably having fun." (Her #1 Value)

Nate "That's great! What kinds of things do I do now, or what things could I do with you or for you, so that you would have the most fun?" (A form of the Sparks Question)

Belinda "I like it when we go to the Family Fun Center together." (Her first Spark for Value #1. I thought that she didn't enjoy going there as much as she used to. I learned that was not the case.)

Nate "What are a couple of other things that have to happen for us to have a lot of fun in our relationship?" (I'm after more Sparks for Value #1.)

Belinda "I love when we go to the beach together and when we travel as a family. I really like it when you and I go clothes shopping together for school." (Three more Sparks for Value #1)

Nate "Is there something I can do almost every day that would be fun for us to do?" (I noticed that the Sparks she was giving me weren't things that I could do almost every day. I wanted to have fun with her on a regular basis.)

Belinda "Hmmm, it's fun when we play our computer games together." (Her fifth Spark for Value #1, one that we can do regularly.)

Nate   "In addition to having fun, what else is important to you in a relationship with a dad?" (Discovering relationship Value #2)

Belinda   "Caring is probably next important." (Her second Value in our relationship)

Nate   "That's neat. What can I do so you know I care about you?" (Discovering her first Spark for Value #2)

Belinda   "I feel that you care about me when you give me good advice." (This one blew my mind! A 12-year-old wanting advice!)

Nate   "What's good advice to you, Belinda?" (I needed to get more clarity on what "good advice" was.)

Belinda   "Good advice is advice that helps me do better."

I went on to discover two more Sparks for Value #2. Then I discovered her third Value for our relationship, which was "love," and elicited four Sparks for that Value.

Next, I wanted to explore her Life Values area. I asked her these questions:

Nate   "Belinda, what's most important to you in life?"

Belinda   "Friends." (I asked the Values Question and she gave me a Spark. I wrote this down as Spark #1 under a yet-to-be-discovered Value.)

Nate   "If you had friends, what would that mean to you?" (I wanted to discover the Value that "having friends" would give her.)

Belinda   "If I had friends, then I would have self-esteem." (Self-esteem is an emotion, so it's her #1 Life Value. I then discovered more Sparks for the self-esteem Value.)

Nate   "In addition to self-esteem, what else is important to you in life?" (I wanted the second Life Value.)

Belinda   "A good education." (She gave me a Spark, so I asked a question that would elevate the Spark to a Value.)

Nate   "What would having a good education give you?"

Belinda   "Success." (Her second Life Value)

At this point we had a nice discussion on all the different ways that she could get a good education—college, reading, talking to people, educational TV, computers, etc. (Notice that the Discovery Process does more than reveal Values and Sparks. It is a valuable tool to help you pinpoint the areas where you need to educate your children.) I went on to discover a third Life Value.

Nate   "What else is important to you in life?"

Belinda   "To be popular." (I had a feeling we would have an interesting discussion here.)

Nate   "What has to happen for you to be popular?" (The Sparks Question)

Belinda   "When everyone likes me." (This is a Spark that is guaranteed to lead to lousy feelings. I knew it was time for some education. After all, Belinda said she wanted "good advice.")

Nate   "Does everyone have to like you for you to be popular?"

Belinda   "Well, I guess not. Just some of the kids would be okay."

Nate   "How important is it to you that they like you for the right reasons? That they like you just because you're a great person?"

Belinda   "Yeah, I guess you're right. Some kids do bad things to try to get liked."

Nate   "So, if you happened to be with a bunch of kids who were taking drugs, and they put pressure on you to take drugs, you could say 'No' and get the heck out of there."

Belinda   "Sure."

Nate   "And if you did that, you would actually have more self-esteem, wouldn't you?" (Her #1 Life Value) "You would be more successful in life, wouldn't you?" (Her #2 Life Value) "And you would still be popular with the right people for the right reasons, wouldn't you?" (Her #3 Life Value)

This is a great example of the power of knowing someone's Values. I could have preached to Belinda about the danger of drugs.

Instead, I chose to link what she wanted most in her life to being drug free.

If you have kids and/or parents, it's time to put your knowledge into action by completing the Exercises for Action below. It's best to do the Values Discovery Process in person, but if you have to use the phone, go for it. Just do it!

EXERCISES FOR ACTION

The Values and Sparks Discovery Process for a Parent/Child Relationship

First, explain to your child why you want to ask these questions. If your child is old enough, study this book together. You might want to review the Additional Insights on pages 75 – 79. Record all of your answers in the back of this book.

A. Explore the Relationship Values Area

1. Ask this Values Question: *"What's most important to you in a relationship with a mom/dad?"* Discover the #1 Value for this area.

2. For the Value you discovered in Step 1 above, ask the Sparks Question, *"What has to happen in order for you to feel (#1 Value)?"* Discover the first Spark for the #1 Value.

3. Discover at least two other Sparks for the #1 Value by asking, *"What else has to happen in order for you to feel (#1 Value)?"*

4. Discover three other Values for the Relationship Values area by asking, *"What else is important to you in a relationship with a mom/dad?"* Then repeat Steps 2 and 3 to discover at least two Sparks for each additional Value you discover.

B. Explore the Life Values Area

1. Ask this Values Question: *"What's most important to you in life?"* Discover the #1 Value for this area.

2. For the Value you discovered in Step 1 above, ask the Sparks Question, *"What has to happen in order for you to feel (#1 Value)?"* Discover the first Spark for the #1 Value.

3. Discover at least two other Sparks for the #1 Value by asking, *"What else has to happen in order for you to feel (#1 Value)?"*

4. Discover at least two other Values for the Life Values area by asking, *"What else is important to you in life?"* Then repeat Steps 2 and 3 to discover at least two Sparks for each additional Value you discover.

Like the television program *Friends*, relationships with real-life friends can be challenging. Fun. A little aggravating (sometimes, a LOT aggravating). But always rewarding.

After you've completed this chapter's Exercises for Action, read on to learn how you can improve your... **Friendships.**

CHAPTER 8

Friendships

*My best friend is the person who
brings out the best in me.*
—Henry Ford

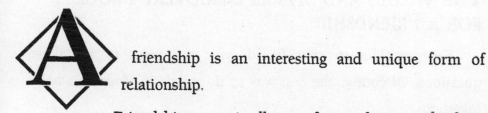 friendship is an interesting and unique form of
relationship.

Friendships come in all sorts of sizes, shapes, and colors.
Some friendships are close. Some are more distant. Some friendships
are new; others are old. In some friendships, you're with the person
frequently. In others, you rarely see the person. Some friendships
were initiated by you and the friend. Others involve a third person
who is "the glue" in the relationship.

Some people have just one type of friend—someone who has similar Values and Sparks to theirs. This requires very little flexibility on the person's part in applying the Diamond Touch because "we're just like two peas in a pod." Having only like-minded friends is certainly better than not having any friends at all, but it's been my experience that having a wide variety of friends expands your horizons. It opens up a whole new world of learning that you would never experience if you just hung around with the same old folks all the time.

▲

In order to have a wide variety of friends, however, you're going to want to be a master of the Diamond Touch.

▼

In order to have a wide variety of friends, however, you're going to want to be a master of the Diamond Touch. Here are the questions to ask to discover your friend's Values and Sparks:

THE VALUES AND SPARKS DISCOVERY PROCESS FOR A FRIENDSHIP

First, explain to your friend why you want to ask these questions. Of course, the best way to do this is to study this book together.

A. Explore the Relationship Values Area

1. Ask this Values Question: *"What's most important to you in a relationship with a friend?"* Discover the #1 Value for this area.

2. For the Value you discovered in Step 1 above, ask the Sparks Question, *"What has to happen in order for you to feel (#1 Value)?"* Discover the first Spark for the #1 Value.

3. Discover at least two other Sparks for the #1 Value by asking, *"What else has to happen in order for you to feel (#1 Value)?"*

4. Discover at least two other Values for the Relationship Values area by asking, *"What else is important to you in a relationship with a friend?"* Then repeat Steps 2 and 3 to discover at least two Sparks for each additional Value you discover.

B. Explore the Life Values Area

1. Ask this Values Question: *"What's most important to you in life?"* Discover the #1 Value for this area.

2. For the Value you discovered in Step 1 above, ask the Sparks Question, *"What has to happen in order for you to feel (#1 Value)?"* Discover the first Spark for the #1 Value.

3. Discover at least two other Sparks for the #1 Value by asking, *"What else has to happen in order for you to feel (#1 Value)?"*

4. Discover at least two other Values for the Life Values area by asking, *"What else is important to you in life?"* Then repeat Steps 2 and 3 to discover at least two Sparks for each additional Value you discover.

One extremely important use of the Value and Sparks Discovery Process is to find out what went wrong after you've upset a friend. Whenever there's been an upset, it means that one or both of you have had your rules broken, i.e., a Spark for a high Value was either ignored or stomped on!

▲

One extremely important use of the Value and Sparks Discovery Process is to find out what went wrong after you've upset a friend.

▼

The following example of the Values and Sparks Discovery Process will illustrate how to discuss an upset and how to open the doors of communication so that you heal the hurt and move forward with the intention of honoring each other's Values and Sparks in the future.

An Example of Using the Values and Sparks Process to Resolve an Upset in a Friendship

Let's assume your friend Tanya told you a story that she wanted you to keep confidential. You didn't realize this and told the story to someone else. Tanya has just confronted you:

Tanya   "I've got a bone to pick with you. Why did you tell Maria what we talked about yesterday?" (She is telling you how a high Value of hers was broken.)

You   "Oh, I'm sorry. I didn't think you'd mind."

Tanya   "Of course I mind. It was personal. I didn't want anybody to know."

You "It sounds like I broke your trust when I told Maria." (You suggest a Value that you believe was violated.)

Tanya "You're darn right!" (Bingo.)

You "I apologize. It wasn't my intent to hurt you. I didn't think you would mind if Maria knew. Let's make sure this doesn't happen again. How can you let me know if our conversation is confidential?" (You clarify the rules of the game. You identify what has to happen for information to be classified as confidential.)

Tanya "I'll tell you if I want some information to be kept confidential." (She tells you what needs to be done differently so her Value of trust is not violated again.)

You "Great. Now I know. In addition, is it okay for me to ask if I think something you tell me may be confidential?" (You add another safeguard to make sure the Value is not violated.)

Tanya "Sure!" (Now, everyone knows the rules of the game.)

As you can see, it doesn't take long to heal upsets if you have the Diamond Touch. When an upset occurs:

1. Identify how the Value was violated.

2. Identify what Value was violated.

3. Identify what needs to be done differently so the violation doesn't happen again. You may need to negotiate this point to reach an agreement that's acceptable to both parties.

The next time you have an upset with someone, use the Diamond Touch and be amazed with the results.

I hope you've done at least one of the Exercises for Action sections in the last two chapters. If you have, the Values and Sparks Discovery Process should be coming more naturally to you. Let's continue the learning process by applying the method to your friendships.

EXERCISES FOR ACTION

The Values and Sparks Discovery Process for a Friendship

First, explain to your friend why you want to ask these questions. Of course, the best way to do this is to study this book together. You might want to review the Additional Insights in Chapter 6, pages 75 – 79. Record all of your answers in the back of this book.

A. Explore the Relationship Values Area

1. Ask this Values Question: *"What's most important to you in a relationship with a friend?"* Discover the #1 Value for this area.

2. For the Value you discovered in Step 1 above, ask the Sparks Question, *"What has to happen in order for you to feel (#1 Value)?"* Discover the first Spark for the #1 Value.

3. Discover at least two other Sparks for the #1 Value by asking, *"What else has to happen in order for you to feel (#1 Value)?"*

4. Discover at least two other Values for the Relationship Values area by asking, *"What else is important to you in a relationship with a friend?"* Then repeat Steps 2 and 3 to discover at least two Sparks for each additional Value you discover.

B. Explore the Life Values Area

1. Ask this Values Question: *"What's most important to you in life?"* Discover the #1 Value for this area.

2. For the Value you discovered in Step 1 above, ask the Sparks Question, *"What has to happen in order for you to feel (#1 Value)?"* Discover the first Spark for the #1 Value.

3. Discover at least two other Sparks for the #1 Value by asking, *"What else has to happen in order for you to feel (#1 Value)?"*

4. Discover at least two other Values for the Life Values area by asking, *"What else is important to you in life?"* Then repeat Steps 2 and 3 to discover at least two Sparks for each additional Value you discover.

You spend approximately 2,000 hours a year at your place of work. Poor work relationships can make even the best job a pain in the neck. Positive work relationships can make going to the office a pleasure. Read on to learn how to use the Diamond Touch in your... **Work Relationships.**

CHAPTER 9

Work Relationships

If you are all wrapped up in yourself,
you are overdressed.
—Kate Halverson

he average American corporation loses half its employees every four years. Here are some interesting statistics on why people leave one company for another. According to a 1996 survey conducted by the Customer Relations Institute of San Diego, the top three reasons for leaving a job were:

1. Frustrating management practices/policies—52%

2. Limited opportunities for growth—13%

3. Low compensation—10%

The top two reasons for leaving a job (almost two-thirds of the total) are directly related to people not having their Values met. Amazingly, only one out of ten people changes jobs for more money! Which goes to prove that *workers value getting their emotional needs met far more than they value money!*

Workers value getting emotional needs met far more than they value money!

Think about your work history—have you ever left a job for another one? Why did you leave? Was it strictly for money, or were there other factors involved?

Now analyze your answer by putting it through the Values and Sparks filter. When your Values are not being met and your Sparks are being broken, you feel pain. What Values were not being met and which Sparks were being broken on the job you left?

When you see an opportunity for your Values and Sparks to be met more completely with a new opportunity (i.e., a new job), you will want to take action to achieve it. In what ways did you see your Values and Sparks being met more completely with the new job? Write the answer in your notebook or journal.

Do you see how your Values and Sparks direct your behavior, and do you see why discovering your work associates' Values and Sparks is so important? When you are an expert at giving others what they want in the way they want it, people will want to be on your team. If you're a leader, they will want to follow you. People will more completely enjoy the 2,000+ hours they spend at work with you each year!

Let's take a minute now and review the Values areas you've explored in the relationships we've covered so far.

With your spouse, you explored two Values areas:

    A. The Relationship with a Spouse Values area

    B. The Life Values area

With your children, you explored two Values areas:

    A. The Relationship with a Mom/Dad Values area

    B. The Life Values area

With your friends, you explored two Values areas:

    A. The Relationship with a Friend Values area

    B. The Life Values area

With your work associates, you will want to explore three Values areas:

    A. The Job/Occupation Values area

    B. The Relationship with an Associate/Manager/Leader Values area

    C. The Life Values area

The Values and Sparks Discovery Process for a Work Relationship

First, explain to your work associate why you want to ask these questions. Of course, the best way to do this is for both of you to study this book together.

A. Explore the Job/Occupation Values Area

1. Ask this Values Question: *"What's most important to you in a job/occupation?"* Discover the #1 Value for this area.

2. For the Value you discovered in Step 1 above, ask the Sparks question: *"What has to happen in order for you to feel (#1 Value)?"*

3. Discover at least two other Sparks for the #1 Value by asking, *"What else has to happen in order for you to feel (#1 Value)?"*

4. Discover at least two other Values for the Job/Occupation Values area by asking, *"What else is important to you in a job/occupation?"* Then repeat Steps 2 and 3 to discover at least two Sparks for each additional Value you discover.

B. Explore the Relationship Values Area

1. Ask this Values Question: *"What's most important to you in a relationship with an associate/manager/leader?"* Discover the #1 Value for this area.

2. For the Value you discovered in Step 1 above, ask the Sparks Question, *"What has to happen in order for you to feel (#1 Value)?"* Discover the first Spark for the #1 Value.

3. Discover at least two other Sparks for the #1 Value by asking, *"What else has to happen in order for you to feel (#1 Value)?"*

4. Discover at least two other Values for the Relationship Values area by asking, *"What else is important to you in a relationship with an associate/manager/leader?"* Then repeat Steps 2 and 3 to discover at least two Sparks for each additional Value you discover.

C. Explore the Life Values Area

1. Ask this Values Question: *"What's most important to you in life?"* Discover the #1 Value for this area.

2. For the Value you discovered in Step 1 above, ask the Sparks Question, *"What has to happen in order for you to feel (#1 Value)?"* Discover the first Spark for the #1Value.

3. Discover at least two other Sparks for the #1 Value by asking, *"What else has to happen in order for you to feel (#1 Value)?"*

4. Discover at least two other Values for the Life Values area by asking, *"What else is important to you in life?"* Then repeat Steps 2 and 3 to discover at least two Sparks for each additional Value you discover.

An Example of Using the Values Discovery Process with a Work Associate

The following is a composite of conversations I've had with work associates through the years.

Nate "Brad, I really like to get to know the people I work with here at XYZ Corporation because everyone has different wants and needs. Would you mind answering a few questions?"

Brad "Sounds good to me."

Nate "What's most important to you in a job?"

Brad "Oh, I don't know. Making lots of money, I guess." (A vague Spark answer)

Nate "If you made lots of money, what would that mean to you?" (I'm asking him to think of his Value for the Spark "making lots of money.")

Brad "That would mean I'm successful." (One of his Values. It may or may not be his highest Value.)

Nate "How much money would you have to make this year to feel like you're successful?" (I'm getting more specific on his Spark for success.)

Brad "$30,000."

Nate "How much are you making now?"

Brad "$25,000." (He's $5,000 short. I know if I can help him move toward making $30,000, I will strengthen our relationship.)

Nate "I've got some ideas of skills you can learn that could lead to an improved income. When we have some more time, we can review a few of them."

Brad "Great!" (People get excited when they feel understood and supported.)

Nate "What else has to happen for you to feel success?" (I'm after his second Spark for success.)

Brad "Hmmmm, I guess being recognized for the good work I do." (His second Spark for the Value of success.)

Nate "There are a lot of ways to be recognized. Which ways are important to you?" (I'm getting very clear on this Spark.)

Brad "It doesn't have to be anything formal, although that's okay. I just like to be told every once in a while that I'm doing a good job."

I could discover more Sparks for the Value of success, but I decide to move on to a second Value.

Nate "In addition to success, what else is important to you in a job?" (I'm after a second Value in the Job Values area.)

Brad "I want a job that challenges me." (Challenge is his second Value.)

Nate   "Of the two things you've mentioned so far—success and challenge—which one is more important to you?" (I want to discover his #1 Value. The order of a person's Values is useful information.)

Brad   "That's a good question."

Nate   "What's a good answer?"

Brad   "Probably challenge."

Nate   "How does a job have to be arranged for it to be challenging?" (Another way of asking for a Spark. It gets tiresome to always ask, "What has to happen in order for you to feel _____?")

Brad   "I need to be constantly learning." (His first Spark for challenge.)

Nate   "What are a few things you would like to learn now that would help you the most? I'll help you learn them as quickly as possible." (I want to discover how I can help him right now. When I do that, I'll have an eager and hard-working associate in my department.)

Brad   "Whoa! You'd do that for me?"

Nate   "Within reason, whenever and wherever I can."

Brad   "I need to learn that new accounting program we use here in the office."

Nate "That's a good first choice. I'll get you enrolled in the next full-day training class. After you're done with the class, we'll talk about the next step."

Brad "I really appreciate your time. Quite frankly, I was kind of skeptical when we first started this."

Nate "I'm glad you like it. Sometime I'll show you how to do it if you want to."

Brad "Let's do it."

Now I'm going to move on to the second Values area—the Relationship with an Associate/Manager/Leader. In this area, we will discover a whole new set of Values and Sparks.

Nate "I'm curious. What's most important to you in a relationship with an associate here at work?"

Brad (He answers very quickly and with a fair amount of intensity.) "Respect." (His first Value for this Values area.)

Nate "That didn't take you long to answer. Did you ever work at a company where you didn't feel respected?" (I knew from the way he answered my last question that he probably had felt disrespected in a previous job.)

Brad "You bet. I quit my last job because I wasn't given any respect."

Nate   "You sound like Rodney Dangerfield. Do you think the problem was with you, them, or both?"

Brad   "What do you mean by that?"

Nate   "Sometimes people have such unrealistic expectations of how other people should act that they're never satisfied no matter what situation they're in."

Brad   "Man, I never thought of it like that. Maybe I have been a little overboard with my expectations."

Nate   "That's just something to think about. In the meantime, what can I do to let you know you're respected?" (Another form of the Sparks Question. Remember, this whole process is much more than a series of specific questions; it's a way of thinking.)

Brad   "When you give me an assignment, don't be constantly looking over my shoulder." (He states his Spark in the negative.)

Nate   "You've told me what you don't want me to do. Tell me what you do want me to do."

Brad   "When you give me an assignment, let me run with it."

Nate   "Be a little more specific. What does 'Let me run with it' mean?"

Brad   "It means that you never bother me about it or ask me how I'm doing." (It looks like some of his unrealistic expectations are beginning to pop up. But better now than later. Just because somebody says that they want to be treated in a certain way doesn't mean that you must do it. As in this case, maybe it would be appropriate to educate the person a little and/or negotiate a plan that's agreeable to both of you.)

Nate   "Brad, I appreciate your independence. We need independent thinkers around here, and I'm responsible for the results of this department. I need to know what's going on so I can help you if I can, and coordinate the efforts of the other people in the department with what you're doing. How can we arrange it so I get the information I need, and you feel respected?"

Brad   "Yeah, I see what you mean. What if I e-mail you a short memo each Friday afternoon outlining what I accomplished during the week?"

Nate   "That sounds fine. I'll be expecting your e-mail update each Friday afternoon. In addition, how about if I just stick my head into your office every week or so to see how you're doing? I'm not trying to be Big Brother or anything. I just want to make sure we're all moving in the same direction. And if you ever want to try something that's in a completely different direction, let me know, and I'll see what I can do. Of course, my door is always open to you if you have any questions or need some resources."

Brad "That sounds fair." (We've negotiated the rules of the game.)

At this point I would move on to discover more of his Values and Sparks for the Relationship with an Associate/Manager/Leader Values area. Then I would discover his Values and Sparks for the Life Values area.

You may have noticed by now that we always start with the least personal Values area and progressively move to more personal Values areas. In this chapter, this is the order we used:

A. the Job/Occupation Values area

B. the Relationship with an Associate/Manager/Leader Values area

C. the Life Values area

Doing it this way allows the person answering the questions to gradually "open up."

In the next week, preferably tomorrow, discover one or more of your work associates' Values and Sparks by completing the Exercises for Action below.

EXERCISES FOR ACTION

The Values and Sparks Discovery Process for a Work Relationship

First, explain to your associate why you want to ask these questions. Of course, the best way to do this is to study this book together. You might want to review the Additional Insights on pages 75 – 79. Record all of your answers in the back of this book.

A. Explore the Job/Occupation Values Area

1. Ask this Values Question: *"What's most important to you in a job/occupation?"* Discover the #1 Value for this area.

2. For the Value you discovered in Step 1 above, ask the Sparks Question, *"What has to happen in order for you to feel (#1 Value)?"* Discover the first Spark for the #1 Value.

3. Discover at least two other Sparks for the #1 Value by asking, *"What else has to happen in order for you to feel (#1 Value)?"*

4. Discover at least two other Values for the Job/Occupation Values area by asking, *"What else is important to you in a job/occupation?"* Then repeat Steps 2 and 3 to discover at least two Sparks for each additional Value you discover.

B. Explore the Relationship Values Area

1. Ask this Values Question: *"What's most important to you in a relationship with an associate/manager/leader?"* Discover the #1 Value for this area.

2. For the Value you discovered in Step 1 above, ask the Sparks Question, *"What has to happen in order for you to feel (#1 Value)?"* Discover the first Spark for the #1 Value.

3. Discover at least two other Sparks for the #1 Value by asking, *"What else has to happen in order for you to feel (#1 Value)?"*

4. Discover at least two other Values for the Relationship Values area by asking, *"What else is important to you in a relationship with an associate/ manager/leader?"* Then repeat Steps 2 and 3 to discover at least two Sparks for each additional Value you discover.

C. Explore the Life Values Area

1. Ask this Values Question: *"What's most important to you in life?"* Discover the #1 Value for this area.

2. For the Value you discovered in Step 1 above, ask the Sparks Question, *"What has to happen in order for you to feel (#1 Value)?"* Discover the first Spark for the #1 Value.

3. Discover at least two other Sparks for the #1 Value by asking, *"What else has to happen in order for you to feel (#1 Value)?"*

4. Discover at least two other Values for the Life Values area by asking, *"What else is important to you in life?"* Then repeat Steps 2 and 3 to discover at least two Sparks for each additional Value you discover.

We've spent the last four chapters learning how to dramatically improve the value of your most precious possession—your relationships—by discovering the Values and Sparks of your spouse… your friends… your children… and your co-workers.

In the next chapter you'll learn about an amazing concept that puts the "polish" on your relationship gems. I call this concept "Creative Giving"—giving in ways that will create a better life for the other person.

If you truly want to "give a gift that keeps on giving"—then turn the page and learn the secret of… **Creative Giving**.

Section 4

When to Give...
and When
to Get

Section 4

When to Give...
and When
to Get

Let's Review:

In the first three sections, you've learned how to apply the Diamond Rule by asking the questions that enable you to discover people's Values and Sparks.

What's Ahead:

In the next chapter, you'll learn the art of Creative Giving—giving in ways that create a better life for the other person and why everyone wins when you give creatively. And in the final chapter, you'll learn about the Power of Giving, including the four levels of giving and how the concept of Giving completes the Cycle of Life.

CHAPTER 10

Creative Giving

Giving, whether it be of time, labor, affection,
advice, gifts, or whatever, is one of
life's greatest pleasures.
—Rebecca Russell

As you've been reading this book, I'll bet you've asked yourself once or twice, "Do I have to give people everything they want right away?"

The answer is a resounding NO!

For example, if your daughter's highest Value in life is success, and her Spark for success is having $1 million in the bank, don't feel obligated to give her a million bucks. Even if you could afford it, handing your daughter a million bucks just because she asked for it wouldn't be in her best long-term interest, wouldn't you agree?

You need to be creative with your giving. A better course of action would be to educate her on the value of taking personal responsibility and the satisfaction that comes from earning money from your own labors, as opposed to having someone give it to you. Then help her learn how to earn and save the money on her own.

▲

The Foundational Rule of Giving: "Give to others in ways that create a better long-term life for them. Give to others in ways that are in their best long-term interest."

▼

To better understand the concept of Creative Giving, let's start with the Foundational Rule of Giving: "Give to others in ways that create a better long-term life for them. Give to others in ways that are in their best long-term interest."

The exact method of giving will vary depending on the nature of the relationship and the goals of the people in the relationship.

CREATIVE GIVING IN ACTION

After you discover someone's Values and Sparks, you have four options:

1. Give with no education or negotiation. In most relationships, this is the option that will occur most frequently. The gift is in the person's best long-term interest, and you can give it easily and gladly. For example, if your son likes to get out the baseball gloves and play catch with you, you can give him that gift on a regular basis with no education or negotiation. You get to spend some quality time together and he improves a skill that will help his contribution to his Little League team.

2. Educate, then give. This option depends on the nature of your relationship with the person. In your opinion, this person may need some education before the gift. This is especially true in parent/child relationships and some work relationships. You may have some knowledge they need in order to make a wiser choice concerning the best Sparks for their Values. For example, let's say you're a manager, and one of your employees wants to be assigned to a certain project team. You may have to educate that person by helping them acquire the skills needed to join the team. You help the employee enroll in a class to learn the skills, and then you assign them to the project team.

3. Negotiate, then give. In all four kinds of relationships covered in Section 3, you may need to negotiate "the rules of the game," that is, you may need to negotiate on the Sparks you can (or want to) give. Be sure to ask the question, "How can we create a win-win situation here?" For example, if your teenage son wants to extend his curfew on weekends from 10 p.m. to midnight, you can negotiate an 11 p.m. curfew. When it comes to negotiation, it's important to remember that both parties can be winners. A great way to accomplish this is to ask a question using the word *and* to connect the wins. For example, In

Chapter 6, a wife asked her husband, "What can I do when I don't like something you've done so that I can get my point across *and* you feel respected?" The husband answered, "You can say you don't like what I just did without making me seem I was wrong. You can ask me not to do something instead of demanding that I don't do it." The husband and wife both win in this negotiation.

4. Don't give. This is your option of choice if you can't give it to them or don't want to give it to them because you don't feel it's in their best long-term interest. Be sure to explain to the person why you don't want to do something. For example, a friend asks you to loan him some money for a new business venture. You don't want to make the loan for any number of reasons. You can say, "No way!" and then explain why.

If you **DO** give, as in A, B, or C, you can do any of the following:

1. Give them all of what they want in the way they want it. This choice usually goes with option A. The playing catch with your son example falls into this category.

2. Give them some of what they want, in the way they want it. This choice usually goes with options B and C. Your reason for not giving them all of what they want should be made clear in the education or negotiation process. The example of curfew negotiation falls into this category.

3. Support or clear the path for their getting what they want, in the way they want it. You may not be the person who actually provides the Sparks for the achievement of their Values. You may elect to support them on their journey to their Values or clear the path to make the journey quicker and safer. The person who wanted to be on the project team example falls into this category.

If you **DO NOT** give it to them (option D), explain why you can't or don't want to and then do any of the following:

4. Accept your Differences in Values and/or Sparks. Agree to disagree. Let's get real—most relationships aren't a perfect match of Values and Sparks. You may want to accept any differences in the rules of the game that can't be resolved. At least you know where the differences lie, which can very enlightening. For example, if your son asks for a midnight curfew, and you believe that this isn't appropriate at his age, you don't have to give it to him or negotiate. Explain why you're making the decision to leave his curfew at 10 p.m. Tell him you love and respect him, and agree to disagree.

If you **DO** give to them with 1, 2, or 3 above, you can make any of these choices:

a. Give now and regularly in the future. If possible and appropriate, provide the Spark so they can feel the emotion and the desire right now! Then give it to them on a regular basis in the future. For example, tell your wife you love her in that certain tone of voice with that "special" embrace right now and every day from now on if that's her Spark for love.

b. Give now and variably in the future. If possible and appropriate, provide the Spark so they can feel the emotion and the desire right now! Then give it to them on a variable basis in the future. Maybe something has to happen first in order for it to be appropriate for you to provide the Spark. Unexpected surprises also have great power. Winning a slot machine jackpot is thrilling because you don't know it's coming. You may choose to provide a Spark at unexpected times to create a special moment. For example, every once in a while, surprise your spouse with a gift that is sure to provide a Spark for them.

c. Give later and regularly in the future. You may not be able to provide the Spark immediately. Do it as soon as possible and regularly in the future. For example, you discover that a client wants telephone conferences with you once a week. If it isn't possible this week, give it to them starting next Tuesday and every Tuesday thereafter.

d. Give later and variably in the future. You may not be able to provide the Spark immediately. Do it as soon as possible and variably in the future for the same reasons as outlined in **b** above. For example, you discover that a friend likes written notes from you. Write the person a note next week and once a month from now on.

On the preceding pages, I've given you many possibilities for giving. The Giving Process Flow Chart on the next page will tie everything together.

THE GIVING PROCESS FLOW CHART

Discover their Values and Sparks

then   or

A. Give with no education   D. Don't give.
   or negotiation.
B. Educate, then give.
C. Negotiate, then give.

and   or

1. Give all of it to them.   4. Accept your differences
2. Give some of it to them.   5. End the relationship.
3. Support or clear the path
   for them.

and

a. Give now and regularly in the future.
b. Give now and variably in the future.
c. Give later and regularly in the future.
d. Give later and variably in the future.

Below are some examples of possible ways of giving. You may want to follow along with the Giving Process Flow Chart. All of the examples are taken from the dialogues in Chapters 6 through 9.

In Chapter 6, a wife discovered that her husband's Relationship Value was respect and his Spark was being hugged and told how proud she was of him. She can now provide the Spark with no education or negotiation. She can do that totally. She can do that now and regularly in the future. This will make him feel loved on a continual basis and probably increase the amount of love he returns to her.

Here's an example from Chapter 7. My daughter, Belinda, has a Value of fun for our relationship. One of her Sparks is playing computer games with me. I can easily provide that Spark with no education or negotiation. I can do that completely. And I can do that right now and once or twice a week at unexpected times in the future.

Here's an example from Chapter 9. I discover that a co-worker's Job Value is success. The Spark for success is earning $30,000 a year. I can give it to him by providing vital learning experiences so he can gain the skills necessary to earn $30,000 a year. I can do that by having a meeting with him next Monday to develop our plan and then meet regularly in the future.

Your second option after you discover people's Values and Sparks is to educate and then give it to them. Here's an example from Chapter 7. As you will recall, my daughter, Belinda, said that self-esteem was one of her Life Values and that education was one of her Sparks. After I discovered that, we had an educating discussion about all the ways she could learn in life. Now I can support her education in the future by regularly helping her with her homework, providing a tutor when needed, and taking her to interesting places.

I also felt some education was in order when she said that being popular was another of her Life Values, and "when everyone likes me" was her Spark. Go back to page 92 now and read this section.

You will see that I tied in "saying no to drugs" with self-esteem and being successful in life (her top two Life Values). You will have tremendous educational impact anytime you show someone that an undesired behavior goes against their stated Values, or that a desired behavior will give them their stated Values.

Your third option after you discover people's Values and Sparks is to negotiate and then give it to them. Here's an example from Chapter 8 on pages 104 – 105. In this example, you broke your friend Tanya's Value of trust. You then negotiated the way you will regularly keep her trust in the future.

The negotiation option also appeared in Chapter 9, on pages 114 – 120 with Nate and Brad in a work situation. We negotiated a way that I could get the information I needed, and Brad could receive the respect he desired.

Which way of giving is the best choice? The answer can be determined by these four questions:

1. What is the right thing to do morally, legally, and ethically?

2. What way of giving is in the person's best long-term interest?

3. Which way of giving will create the best life for the person?

4. Which way of giving supports my goals, dreams, and way of life? Consider your capacity for giving. If you over-give to too many people, you may lose in the long·run because it will decrease your ability to give in the future when it's truly needed.

Remember, you won't always be perfect in your giving. Give, evaluate the results, and modify your giving. Effective giving is an art that takes experience to master. Now, you can continue your mastery of the Diamond Rule by completing the Exercises for Action on the next page.

EXERCISES FOR ACTION

Record your answers in the back of this book.

1. If you're married, discover your mate's Values and Sparks and then create a plan for giving it to them using the information in this chapter.

2. If you're in a parent/child relationship, discover the person's Values and Sparks and then create a plan for giving it to them using the information in this chapter.

3. In one of your friendships, discover the person's Values and Sparks and then create a plan for giving it to them using the information in this chapter.

4. In one of your work relationships, discover the person's Values and Sparks and then create a plan for giving it to them using the information in this chapter.

CHAPTER 11

The Power of Giving

◇

You cannot hold a torch to light another's path
without brightening your own.

—Ben Sweetland

◇ n the last chapter, you learned about the Foundational Rule of Giving—"Give to others in ways that create a better long-term life for them."

In this chapter, I hope you will come to more fully appreciate the immense power that is released when a gift is given and received. That power is increased as you move down the four levels of giving.

THE FOUR LEVELS OF GIVING

1. *Level One*—The receiver loses, and the giver wins. **The giver is a con artist.**

2. *Level Two*—The receiver wins, and the giver loses. **The giver is a martyr.**

3. *Level Three*—The receiver wins, and the giver wins. **The giver is a true friend.**

4. *Level Four*—The receiver wins, the giver wins, and other people win. **The giver is a team player.**

Let's take a closer look at each one of these levels to discover where you might be right now in your giving... compared to where you'd like to be.

Level One—The receiver loses, and the giver wins. The giver is a con artist.

In reality, Level One isn't giving at all. It's taking under the guise of giving. All con artists take advantage of people by pretending to be givers. This can be done intentionally or unintentionally, but the result is the same.

Here is an example of unintentional Level One giving. Some financially rich parents give large sums of money to their children when the kids are still young. This makes the parents feel like winners because they think it says, "We'll do everything we can to help the kids." But does the gift truly help the children in the long run? Usually not, because it robs them of their incentive to learn, grow, and work hard for their own success. The kids become complacent, thinking, "We've got it made. We don't have to work."

Here's an example of intentional Level One giving. Some people don't feel good about themselves, and to make themselves feel better, they give other people the "gift" of put-downs and criticism. If accepted, those gifts tear other people down.

Likewise, con artists build themselves up by tearing others down—deliberately and often with an elaborate plan. Usually, they are exposed sooner or later. When this happens, they move on to a new "victim." Con artists seem to be winning in the short haul; they always lose in the end, however.

Are there any areas of your life where you are unconsciously being a Level One giver? The feeling of guilt is a signal that this is happening. Or other people may tell you that your "gift" doesn't feel like a gift. Remember, just because you think you're a giver doesn't mean you are one. The receiver is the final authority of what is truly a gift.

Level Two—The receiver wins, and the giver loses. The giver is a martyr.

Level Two is probably an improvement over Level One. The giver truly helps the other person, but gives so much or gives in such inappropriate ways that they're hurt in the long run. This may seem admirable, but martyr-like giving decreases the ability to give in the future because there is little left to give.

Sometimes parents who work outside the home fall into the martyr category. They give to their spouses. They give to their children. They give to their employer. They give to their organizations. They give to their community. Then, at the end of the day, there's no time or energy left for themselves. As a result, they don't take care of themselves physically, emotionally, or spiritually, which can lead to burnout or the "Is This All There Is?" Syndrome. The best thing martyrs can do is to pull back on some of their giving so they have the ability to keep on giving in the long run.

You also may want to examine your life for any instances of Level Two giving. A sure sign of this is feeling unfulfilled after you give. I had this happen in my life about a year ago. As a speaker, trainer, and consultant, I'm asked on numerous occasions to give free presentations to not-for-profit groups such as Head Start, Job Corps, schools, prisons, and civic groups. I was doing about twenty of these presentations a year. I love giving to these groups, but on a long plane ride home from one of these presentations, I was feeling resentful about it. I'd been away from my family too much, and I didn't feel good about that. I wasn't making much progress with this book, and I was frustrated with that.

So I made the decision to limit myself to eight free presentations each year. Three of them had to be in the San Diego area where I live. My decision has worked out well. I'm much more discriminating about who I do presentations for, and I feel good about each one I do. There will probably be a time in my life when I will want to increase the number, but for now, eight per year is the right number for me.

Level Three—The receiver wins, and the giver wins. The giver is a true friend.

In Level Three, there are no losers. The giver and receiver both benefit. This book is full of examples of Level Three giving. When I take my daughter to the Family Fun Center, that's Level Three giving. When I provide excellent service to a client, that's Level Three giving.

With Level Three giving, both parties benefit because the act of giving provides energy to a series of events I call the Cycle of Life. The Cycle of Life is described in detail below. To make it more personal, let's make you the giver.

The Cycle of Life

The Cycle of Life has four stages: **BE, DO, HAVE,** and **GIVE.**

BEing is where it all begins—when you are BEing resourceful… happy… or loving, for example, you will DO resourceful, happy, or loving things.

DO is the second stage of the Cycle of Life. Much of our lives is spent DOing things, but we have to ask ourselves whether we're DOing the things that are meaningful, that will make a difference for ourselves and others. If your actions, your DOing, arise from empowering states of BEing, you will naturally choose to DO what is meaningful and important.

HAVE is the third stage of the Cycle of Life. *Most people focus almost exclusively on the HAVE stage, and forget they have to BE and DO first!* When you consistently DO the right things, you will HAVE the things you desire in life. You will HAVE all the relationships, emotions, skills, and possessions that accompany a life well lived.

Now that you HAVE what you desire, you can't stop there—you must move to the fourth stage of the cycle. You must GIVE from what you HAVE. And more important than giving anything material, you must GIVE to others your positive emotional states, like happiness and love. You must GIVE away your support and knowledge. And yes, when appropriate, you may choose to GIVE your physical and financial assets, as well. Your goal in giving should always be to enable the recipients to BE, DO, and HAVE more in their own lives. When the giving is done precisely because you have accurately discovered the other person's Values and Sparks, you are truly practicing the Diamond Rule.

Giving is a vital part of the Cycle of Life for two reasons. First, you will receive from life that which you give. When you give support, happiness, and love, for example, you will receive support, happiness, and love in your life because you will attract people and experiences that will enhance these positive emotions inside you.

When you reflect a resourceful attitude to the world, you will attract the very resources you need—whether they be physical, emotional, or spiritual—that will move you toward your personal vision. When you give happiness, you will attract it; when you give love, you become a magnet for all the love in the world. And these gifts of life will enhance your BEing, and the Cycle of Life can begin anew with even greater power!

Second, when you master the Diamond Rule and GIVE to others in empowering ways, they will never BE the same. You will help enhance their BEing, and a new improved Cycle of Life will begin for them, allowing them to DO and HAVE more—and GIVE more to others, as well. Your Cycles of Life become connected. It looks like this:

The Interdependent Cycles of Life

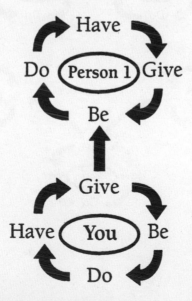

Level Four—The receiver wins, the giver wins, and other people win. The giver is a team player.

▲

At Level Four, the receiver wins, you win, and other people win.

▼

Level Four is the highest level at which you can play the giving game. At Level Four, the receiver wins, you win, and other people win. This is nothing more than connecting numerous Cycles of Life together to create one ever-expanding Upward Spiral of Life.

The Upward Spiral of Life

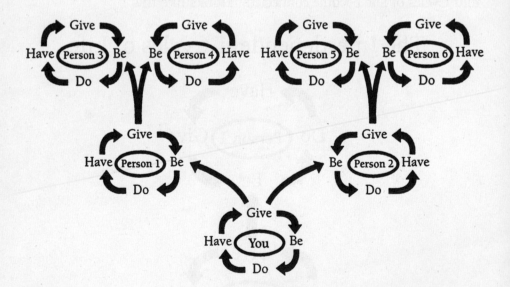

148

Here's a simple yet revealing example of creating an Upward Spiral of Life. As part of my travels, I take taxis in most cities I visit. I have two basic choices when I'm in the cab. I can ignore the driver and stay in my own world. Or I can have a meaningful conversation with the driver and learn from his experience—which is almost always vastly different from my own. During the conversation I can always give the driver the gift of respect and appreciation. I ask about his or her experiences in life (often experiences gained in a different country). I ask for opinions of our country and us as a people. I ask, "What's one thing we Americans could learn from the people in your native country?"

At the end of the ride, I always give a nice tip, and just as important, I look the driver in the eye, shake hands, and say, "I appreciate the great service and the information you gave me." If they act interested in what I'm doing, I like to give drivers a copy of one of my books.

This is Level Four giving because:

1. The other person wins by receiving the gifts of respect and appreciation that enhance BEing.

2. I win. I enjoy seeing drivers come alive as they talk with me. You should see the change in their faces from the beginning to the end of the ride.

3. Do you think it stops here? How do drivers treat the next person in the cab? Perhaps a little bit better. How do they treat their families when they go home? Perhaps a little bit better.

149

Maybe they'll even read the book to gain some knowledge that will make their lives and the lives of the people they care about better. In short, other people will win as a result of my gift.

When it comes to Level Four giving, you might be thinking, "But there is so much I want to do. Where do I start?" Start with yourself. As Mahatma Gandhi said, "We must become the change we seek in the world." Create a BEing who has enormous spiritual, emotional, physical, and even financial riches. Then create an attitude of giving. Look for places in all areas of your life where you can give at Levels Three and Four.

After you have created your personal treasure chest of gifts, begin giving to those closest to you—your spouse, your children, your parents, and your siblings. Bob and Elizabeth Dole were right in the 1996 presidential campaign. As they said often, "It takes a family." The most precious gifts of all are the ones given to your family.

▲

The most precious gifts of all are the ones given to your family.

▼

After you have given to your family, you can begin to give to those in your community. Are there people in your city or neighborhood who could benefit from your gifts of time, attention, and money? If so, give to them on a regular basis. It's up to you how big you want to make your community—how many Cycles of Life you want to affect. As our world gets smaller, our community gets bigger, and our challenges and opportunities increase.

There's another piece of the puzzle that we need to explore. For every giver, there is a receiver. How good are you at receiving? Do you make it easy for others to jump-start their Cycle of Life by giving to you? If you don't, you're being selfish.

For instance, a few years ago, I noticed that I was not fully accepting people's compliments. They would give me praise for a presentation, and I would get embarrassed, look away, and say, "Oh, I don't know about that," or "You probably say that to everybody." Then I began thinking, "Who wins when I say that?" Nobody wins. I was being selfish. Now, when people give me a compliment, I look them right in the eye and say, "Thank you. I really appreciate your saying that!" They win. I win. Everyone's Cycle of Life flows a little faster and smoother.

I challenge you to take your level of giving and receiving to a higher level. Then when you practice the Diamond Rule, your life will flow with ease, creating deep relationships that prosper and endure. And always remember: Quality relationships—like quality diamonds—*are forever!*

Conclusion

The Fable of
the Diamond
Windows

The Fable of the Diamond Windows

It often happens that I wake up at night and begin to think about a serious problem and decide I must tell the President about it. Then I wake up completely and remember that I am the President.

—Harry Truman
33rd president of the United States

I was sitting on a plane when I overheard a conversation between a little girl and her mother. The little girl was telling her mom about a book she read in school. The story is a fitting closing to a book about the Diamond Rule.

Here's her story:

A little girl lived with her mother and father in an apartment on the top floor of an old building in New York City. The father worked as a cab driver. The mother was a homemaker. The family didn't have much—not even a color TV. So the little girl spent a lot of her time looking out her bedroom window.

She watched the people on the street below her and imagined where they worked. She watched the cabs zip by and imagined where the passengers were heading. She watched the policemen direct traffic and imagined what they were shouting to the drivers.

But most of all she stared at the top floor of the apartment building down the block from her. It was her favorite thing to look at because the apartment had *diamond windows!*

"How lucky they must be to live in an apartment with diamond windows," she thought to herself. "Just look at the way the sun sparkles off the diamonds, shooting blue and white beams all over the city. I'd give anything to live in an apartment with diamond windows."

One day the little girl's aunt came to visit. "Let's go for a walk," the aunt said to the little girl. "Where would you like to go?"

"Can we visit the building with the diamond windows?" the little girl asked.

"Of course," smiled the aunt. "You lead the way."

The little girl tugged and pulled her aunt down the stairs... across the street... and down the sidewalk... until she was directly beneath the apartment with the diamond windows. But as she looked up, all she saw was dirty glass instead of diamonds.

The diamonds had disappeared!

Suddenly, another little girl exited the apartment building.

"Why are you staring at my apartment?" the other girl asked.

"I'm looking for the diamond windows. I can see them gleaming in the sun from my bedroom. What did you do with the diamonds?"

"I don't have diamond windows," she replied. "My windows are made of glass. And most of the time the glass is dirty. If you want to see the apartment with diamond windows, look over your shoulder. It's right over there!"

The little girl turned and looked down the block. Sure enough, there was an apartment with diamond windows. Then the little girl gasped. The diamond windows she was staring at were in her building. In fact, the diamond windows *were her own bedroom windows!*

The little girl headed back to her apartment. From time to time, she'd glance up at her bedroom and watch the sun sparkle off her diamond windows. She took her time returning home. She smiled at everyone who passed by. The little girl knew she was the luckiest person in the world. *For she lived in a home with diamond windows!*

◇ ◇ ◇

When you think about it, we all live in homes with diamond windows. It's not the windows that make the diamonds—*it's our perspective!*

You see, we look at other people's lives *from the outside.* From the outside, it looks to us as if other peoples' lives sparkle and shine like diamonds. We mistake the sunlight reflecting off the glass window for diamonds, and we envy others' good fortune.

When you think about it, we all live in homes with diamond windows.

But we look at our own lives from the opposite perspective. We look at our own lives *from the inside.* As a result, all we see are smudges on the glass and dust on the window sills. "If only I had diamond windows like the people down the block," we say to ourselves. "Then I would be happy once and for all."

The simple truth is, the diamond windows that all of us seek aren't down the block. True happiness and true wealth aren't down the block. They reside within!

We don't need to change houses to discover our diamond windows. We just need to change our perspective! We just need to step mentally outside ourselves and look at our lives from a fresh viewpoint. Only then can we can see that the diamond windows have been right in our own homes!

Our diamond windows are reflected in the dining room mirror when we're eating dinner with our family.

Our diamond windows are reflected in the car windshield when we're driving to a friend's house.

Our diamond windows are reflected in the stained-glass of the church we attend each Sunday.

My friend, you don't need to go down the block in search of diamond windows. The diamonds of your life—your relationships— have been right in front of you all along!

I challenge you to look at your relationships from a new perspective.

I challenge you to appreciate the value... beauty... and uniqueness of each of your relationships.

But most of all, I challenge you to begin the process of cutting… and shaping… and polishing your most precious possession until they sparkle and shine like never before, now that you have learned… *the secrets of a Master Diamond Cutter!*

NOTES

NOTES

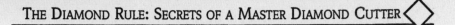

NOTES

NOTES

NOTES

NOTES